STAUNINGS ALPS

Expedition Guide

THE EXPEDITION LIBRARY

*Expedition guides in this series
are planned for major mountain
areas and ranges in the Andes
Africa and Himalaya*

THE EXPEDITION LIBRARY

General Editor: Louis C. Baume

Staunings Alps - Greenland

SCORESBY LAND AND NATHORSTS LAND

Donald J. Bennet

GASTON'S ALPINE BOOKS

WEST COL PRODUCTIONS

First published in Great Britain jointly by
Gaston's Alpine Books and West Col Productions
1 Meadow Close, Goring, Reading, Berks. RG8 OAP

SBN 901516 58 9

Acknowledgements

Many climbers and others have helped in the pre-
paration of this book. In particular I would like to
thank Bill Brooker for his contribution on the
geology of Scoresby Land, and Edna Stewart for
making her notes on the flora available to me.
Several climbers have made their records and
knowledge freely available, and for their assistance
I thank Erik Hoff, Claude Rey, Hermann Huber,
Malcolm Slesser, Mike Fleming, Dewi Jones, Roger
Allen, Iain Smart, Roger Nisbet, Dick Palmer, Keith
Miller, Geoffrey Halliday and Harry Pinkerton.

Printed in England by
Cox & Wyman Ltd, London, Reading and Fakenham

Contents

Editor's Note	7
Scoresby Land and the Staunings Alps	9
Geography and Glaciers	13
Approaches	21
Mountaineering	28
History of the Exploration	32
List of Mountains Climbed	54
List of Passes	78
Future Climbing Prospects	82
Nathorsts Land	86
Geology of Scoresby Land and the Staunings Alps	89
Fauna of Scoresby Land	92
Flora of Scoresby Land	97
Information for Expedition Planning	99
1. Travel	
2. Weather	
3. Equipment	
4. Food	
Specimen Food and Equipment List	109
Explanatory Notes	111
Bibliography	113
Index	117

ERRATUM

Page 14, line 17 should read:

"of the Frihedstinde. The scenery of the Vikingebrae is spec–"

Illustrations

PLATES (between pages 60-61)

1. Camp in the upper basin of the Lang Gletscher. *D. J. Bennet*
2. North Face of the Bersaerkertinde. *R. Chalmers*
3. Near head of the Bersaerkerbrae. *R. Chalmers*
4. Looking towards head of the Sefstroms Glacier. *D. J. Bennet*.
5. An unclimbed spire near the Sefstromsgipfel. *C. F. Knox*
6. Attilaborgen. *D. J. Bennet*
7. Kong Oscars Fjord. *D. J. Bennet*
8. Norsketinde from the south. *E. Hofer*
9. Emmanuel, Sidney and Sussex peaks. *E. Hoff*

MAPS

1. Scoresby Land in East Greenland, *page 8*
2. Principal Glaciers of the Staunings Alps, *page 12*
3. Approaches to East Greenland, *page 100*

in pocket at back of book
4. North and Central Staunings Alps
5. South and Central Staunings Alps

The last two maps are also sold separately as a pair

Editor's Note

Though a certain amount of information on the Staunings Alps has been published in a number of different books and journals during the last twenty years, this information has never been collated and put together between the covers of one book.

It seemed an appropriate choice, therefore, to publish this knowledge – corrected, brought up to date, and completed with a whole lot of new information – as the first volume in the new Expedition Library, which will be devoted to the remoter areas now coming within the reach of the average mountaineering organisations and parties.

We are indebted to Donald Bennet for having undertaken this work and for having prepared with such care the detailed maps which accompany it. Mr Bennet had been to the Staunings Alps on no less than three occasions and so he knew the subject and the terrain intimately.

Naturally, in new territory such as this – opened up only relatively recently by a number of uncoordinated parties from different countries – it takes time for the definitive surveys to be completed and for the multifarious names given to the glaciers and mountains to be considered and approved finally by the appropriate Danish authorities.

The information brought back by these different parties is sometimes scanty and occasionally, and inevitably, conflicting. Many peaks have been given more than one name, and the same name has been given on occasions to more than one peak; the exact positions of several named peaks are uncertain. Despite these difficulties, Mr Bennet has succeeded in putting together all this scattered information and thus in presenting an accurate and complete account, which not only records in a logical sequence the achievements of past expeditions but also provides a very sound basis for the planning of future expeditions.

It must be emphasised, however, that nearly all the heights given are approximate – some are more approximate than others – and that the names used for glaciers and mountains are not necessarily those that have been or will be approved finally by the Geodetic Institute of Denmark.

Louis Baume

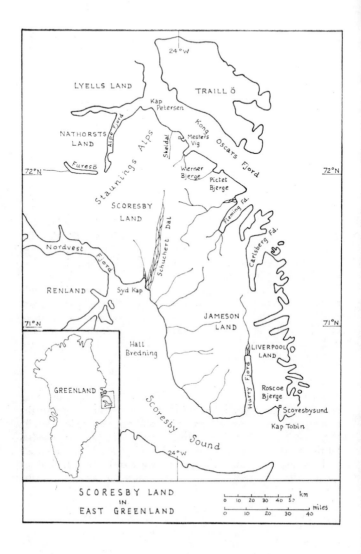

SCORESBY LAND
IN
EAST GREENLAND

Scoresby Land and the Staunings Alps

Scoresby Land, together with neighbouring Jameson Land and Liverpool Land, is a large peninsula on the east coast of Greenland between latitudes 70°N and 73°N. The 24°W line of longitude passes through the centre of the peninsula, which is about 200km. from north to south, and about 100km. wide from east to west (Map 1).

On its seaward side the peninsula is bounded on the north by Alpe Fjord and Kong Oscars Fjord, on the east by the open waters of the Arctic Ocean, and on the south and south-west by Scoresby Sound and Nordvest Fjord which together form the largest and one of the grandest of all the Greenland fiords. It is 325km. long and icebergs calving off the great inland glaciers drift slowly down the fiord towards the sea, some of them one km. in length and rising 100m. above the water.

The Scoresby Land peninsula is one of the largest single parts of Greenland lying outwith the ice-cap which covers ninety per cent of the island. Much of the peninsula consists of low-lying tundra and gravel covered hills. The Skel and Schuchert valleys, which run more or less north to south along the 24°W line of longitude, divide the land into two parts whose characteristics are quite different. East of the valleys the land is mostly low rolling hills, almost devoid of vegetation, with three higher mountain groups rising to 1600 or 1700m. These are the Werner Bjerge and the Pictet Bjerge in the north, and the mountains of the Liverpool Coast in the extreme south-east.

On the west of the Skel and the Schuchert valleys is the magnificent mountain range called the Staunings Alps. Here there are literally hundreds of distinct mountains – snow domes, rock spires, huge walls and narrow ridges. About twelve of these mountains exceed 2700m. the highest being the Dansketinde (2930m.) and there are many others between 2400 and 2700m. high. The highest and grandest part of the Staunings Alps is in the northern half of the range, that part lying just north of latitude 72°N in the northern tip of Scoresby Land between Alpe Fjord and Kong Oscars Fjord. South and west of this area the mountains become slightly lower and less steeply individualistic, until at about longtitude 26°W, in the area of the Prinsesse Gletscher and the Borgbjerg Gletscher, they gradually merge into the main Greenland ice-cap, whose eastern promontories reach this line. The south-eastern outliers of the Staunings Alps drop gradually to Scoresby Sound and the wide lower reaches of the Schuchert Dal (Dal = valley).

Scoresby Land is for the most part uninhabited. The only settlement of any size is at Scoresbysund, near Kap Tobin at the south-eastern tip of the peninsula. Here there is a small community of Greenlanders (as the Eskimos in this part of the arctic are now known) and Danes living in modern, recently built timber houses. The principal occupation of the Greenlanders is hunting but the community is economically non-viable and is supported by Denmark. There is a small airstrip at Scoresbysund and ships from Denmark call with supplies when the state of the pack-ice permits. Until recently there was a much smaller settlement at Syd Kap on the north shore of Scoresby Sound, near the foot of the Schuchert Dal, but this is now deserted.

The only other settlement in Scoresby Land is at Mesters Vig, on the north-east coast of the peninsula about 50km. south-east of its northern tip, Kap Petersen. At Mesters Vig there is a long gravel airstrip, and radio and meteorological stations. One km. from the airstrip there is a harbour of sorts, and usually at least one ship each year calls in July or August.

Fifteen years ago Mesters Vig was also the site of a busy mine. This was situated 10km. inland in a stony valley called the Tunnelelv, surrounded by even stonier hills. Rich ores of lead and zinc were mined from these hills, and processed before being shipped to Europe; however, the cost and difficulty of shipping through the pack-ice (which in some years made it possible for only one or two ships to get through) caused the enterprise to be abandoned about 1960. Now the remains of the mine and the huts that once housed about a hundred workers throughout the year stand silent and deserted among the stony hills, reminiscent of a North American ghost town after an unsuccessful gold rush.

Other mining and prospecting operations have been carried out in Scoresby Land in the last ten or fifteen years. At Malmberg, high up in the Schuchert Dal, there are the remains of another mine where once molybdenum was extracted from an incredibly steep rock peak on the western edge of the Werner Bjerge. Now the huts of Malmberg are toppling over as the snows of successive winters bear down on them, and the glacier below the mine is littered with hundreds of oil drums and other debris of technology. However, for a month or two each summer geologists and prospectors of the Nordisk Mineselskab live and work there, searching the surrounding hills and valleys for valuable minerals.

The camp and airstrip at Mesters Vig are under the control of the Greenland Ministry of the Danish Government and about twenty people, nearly all Danes, live and work there. The airstrip is now used only infrequently by Danish military aircraft on ice patrol, by helicopters of the Nordisk Mineselskab on prospecting operations, and by occasional aircraft bringing supplies to the camp and climbers to the Staunings Alps. From the mountaineers' point of view, Mesters Vig is important because of its nearness to the Staunings Alps, whose eastern outliers are less than twenty miles (35km) away, and because it can be reached in less than six hours flying time from Scotland.

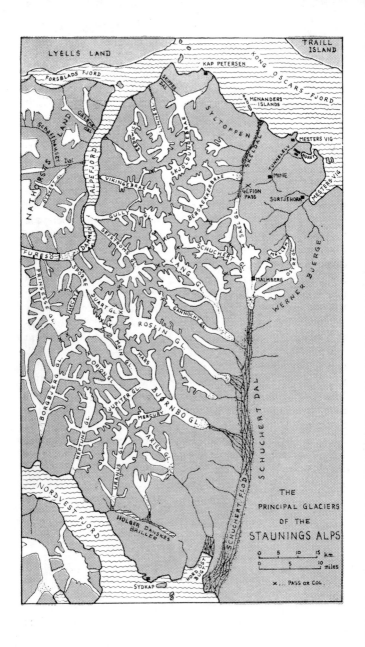

THE

PRINCIPAL GLACIERS

OF THE

STAUNINGS ALPS

0   5   10   15 km.

0   5   10 miles

×... PASS OR COL.

Geography and Glaciers

The geography of the Staunings Alps can probably best be appreciated by observing the directions of the principal glaciers, some of which are 40km. long or more (Map 2).

In the North and Central Staunings the glaciers radiate outwards from the heart of the range. Thus the Sefstroms Glacier, Gully Gletscher and Vikingebrae flow westwards into Alpe Fjord. The Skjoldungebrae flows north to Kap Petersen, and the Bersaerkerbrae flows north-east into the Skeldal. Finally the Schuchert, Lang and Gannochy glaciers flow south-east into the Schuchert Dal.

In the west and south Staunings the comparatively short Spörre and Prinsesse glaciers flow north into the Furesö, and the huge Roslin, Bjørnbo and Borgbjerg glaciers flow southeast or south into the Schuchert Dal or the Nordvest Fjord.

The heart of the range (if so complex a group of mountains can have a single focal point) is probably Col Major, (marked on some maps as Majorpasset), the pass between the Gully Gletscher and the Bersaerkerbrae. Certainly Col Major is in the centre of the highest and grandest peaks, and it is the key to the direct traverse through the mountains from Mesters Vig to the head of the Alpe Fjord.

The source of the Bersaerkerbrae is the steep ice gully which plunges down 500m. on the east side of Col Major. From there the Bersaerkerbrae flows east and then north-east to the Skeldal, a total distance of about 25km. For the most part the glacier is easy, with two very small icefalls and one or two crevassed areas. Early in the summer it is an unbroken highway of ice and snow. Of its side glaciers, none of which is large, the biggest is the Dunottar Glacier whose two branches enclose the peak of Dunottar on the north-west side of the Bersaerkerbrae. The north branch of the Dunottar Glacier has what appears to be an easy pass at its head leading over to the Skjoldungebrae.

The source of the Skjoldungebrae is about 4km. north of Col Major, and the glacier flows northwards for about 35km. until it divides to form two outflows near Kap Petersen. Like the Bersaerkerbrac it is easy for most of its length and has numerous small side glaciers.

West of the Skjoldungebrae, between it and Alpe Fjord, are three smaller glaciers in the group of mountains called the Murchison Bjerge. The Linne Gletscher is parallel to, but shorter than, the Skjoldungebrae, and the Sedgwick and Fangshytte glaciers are smaller and connected by an easy pass which leads from one to the other.

The Vikingebrae, although only about 20km. long, is one of the most spectacular of the Staunings glaciers. It rises on the north side of the Dansketinde and drops steeply in two big icefalls to its level lower reaches. Here an important side-glacier joins it from the Friheds Pass on the north-west side of the most spectacular of the Staunings glaciers. It rises on tacular, in particular the range of mountains on its south side which culminates in the Norsketinde and the Dansketinde.

South of the Vikingebrae, and parallel to it, is the Gully Gletscher. This must rank as the finest of the Staunings glaciers on three counts: it is surrounded by some of the highest and finest of the Staunings peaks, it has three large and difficult icefalls in its 25km. length, and it shares with the Sefstroms Glacier its final spectacular plunge into Alpe Fjord. The ascent of the Gully Gletscher is a serious undertaking and its three icefalls can pose considerable problems of route finding and technical difficulty. The first icefall is usually bypassed by the steep snow and occasional rock on the south side. The second icefall is easier and can usually be climbed near the middle. The third icefall, a chaotic jumble of crevasses and seracs, is the least predictable and the route through it must depend on prevailing conditions. The upper basin of the glacier is open and smooth compared with the narrow lower reaches, and leads to three passes of which Col Major has already been described. On the Gully side this col is easy, and gentle snow slopes lead up to the precipitous drop overlooking the Bersaerkerbrae.

South-west of Col Major is the fine isolated mountain, Bolvaerket, whose narrow ridges rise abruptly from the snows of
the Gully Gletscher. On both sides of Bolvaerket there are
cols between the Gully and Lang glaciers. Crescent Col on
the east is an easy pass on both sides, being little more than
gentle snow slopes. The col on the west of Bolvaerket looks
much more formidable, and there is no record of a crossing.

Between the Vikingebrae and the Gully Gletscher are two
narrow glaciers, the Vertebrae and the Invertebrae, which
are linked by the Wordie Pass and form an interesting traverse between the two big glaciers. There are icefalls on both
glaciers and so the crossing is not altogether easy. The Vertebrae joins the Gully Gletscher on its north side just above
the second icefall; on the opposite side the Cavendish Glacier, which has its source on the north-west side of the Korsspids, plunges down in a huge icefall to join the Gully.

The Sefstroms Glacier is 25km. long and is probably
second only to the Gully Gletscher among the glaciers of the
Staunings. Ascending the glacier from Alpe Fjord, the first
15km. are smooth and easy but the mountains on both sides
are in stark contrast to the nearly level glacier. The soaring
peak of the Sefstromstinde, rising over 2000m. in a single
sweep of rock and ice, the great wedge of Attilaborgen and
the spires of Kastenberg all combine to create a magnificent
mountain setting. About 15km. up the Sefstroms is the
confluence of its three tributaries – the Cantabrae, the Grantabrae and the upper part of the Sefstroms Glacier itself.

The head of the Cantabrae is linked to the Roslin Gletscher by the Newnham Col, a fairly easy pass surrounded by
magnificent mountains about 2700m. high – Trinity, Snetoppen and Cantabrigia. The Grantabrae is separated from the
Lang Gletscher by the rock wall which forms the Grantalang Col; and at the head of the Sefstroms a hitherto un-
crossed pass leads south-east into a tributary of the Lang
Gletscher.

South-west of the Sefstroms Glacier is the Krabbe Gletscher, a short and contorted glacier whose snout (a jumble of

tottering seracs) drops into the head of Dammen between two pincer-like moraines which almost form a small lagoon. The entire glacier is steep and broken, a succession of minor icefalls, and there are no easy cols at its head. The only known route up the glacier is on the screes and ledges of the true left flanking wall.

Next comes the Spörre Gletscher. The snout and terminal moraine of this glacier is a 5km. wilderness of boulders, gravel and dirty ice which forms a barrier between Dammen and the Furesö. The lower part of the glacier is a long icefall, whose difficulty (according to all reports) varies from year to year. About 10km. up, the Duart Glacier joins the Spörre; the upper reaches of both these glaciers are broad and fairly easy, although the area near their confluence is crevassed. The head of the Spörre Gletscher is a vast high-level snowfield surrounded by peaks which rise only 400 to 600m. from the glacier. The upper part of the Duart Glacier is heavily crevassed but the pass at its head is easy and leads over to the Roslin Gletscher. Three fairly large glaciers – Castor, Pollux and Hecate – join the Spörre on its west side below the confluence with the Duart Glacier.

West of the Spörre Gletscher is the Prinsesse Gletscher, which plunges directly into the dark waters of the Furesö. The glacier is about 25km. long and is for the most part straight, narrow and deeply enclosed by mountains. On the west side of the glacier the enclosing mountains are really the edge of the ice-cap. At the head of the glacier there are possible cols which might lead over to the Spörre and Borgbjerg glaciers.

Returning to the north-east corner of the Staunings, the Skel Glacier flows north from the Skel Pass, and a few km. above its snout it is joined by two tributaries on the west side. The Edinbrae descends abruptly into the Skel in a large icefall, while the Kishmul Glacier flows more smoothly to join the main ice stream. At the head of the Edinbrae an easy pass leads over to the Schuchert Gletscher; there is also an easy pass, the Glamis Col, between the Kishmul Glacier and the Bersaerkerbrae.

On the south-east of the Staunings all glaciers flow into the Schuchert Dal whose bottom is a broad expanse of mud, sand and gravel intersected by fast flowing streams.

The Schuchert Gletscher itself has its source near the centre of the range about 3km. south-east of Col Major. There appears to be a fairly easy pass from the head of the Schuchert to the upper snowfields of the Gully Gletscher, but there is no record of any crossing. About 5km. down the glacier there is a fairly easy col, the Trumpington Col, which leads from a small side glacier on the south-west side of the Schuchert over to the broad upper basin of the Lang Glets-cher. The Schuchert is wide and smooth for its whole length of about 30km., and the snout of the glacier is eventually lost under a wilderness of boulders and scree which forms its terminal moraine.

The Lang Gletscher (named Stor Gletscher on some maps) has its source at the Crescent Col and flows south-east for about 30km. The upper part of the glacier is a wide snow basin surrounded by some magnificent mountains, of which Bolvaerket and its outliers are probably the grandest. In the north-west corner of this basin Churchill Col gives access to the Kirkbrae, a tributary of the Sefstroms Glacier. Lower down the Lang narrows and is joined by several large tri-butaries. First, on its south-west side a very big unnamed (and unexplored) glacier enters the Lang; then another un-named glacier joins it from the north-east; finally, near the snout, the long and narrow Gannochy Glacier joins the Lang. The head of the Gannochy is connected to the Dalmore Gla-cier by the Courier Pass.

The Roslin Gletscher is one of the biggest of all the Staun-ings glaciers, being almost 55km. long. Throughout its length it is broad and gentle. At its source an easy pass leads over to the Duart Glacier, and a few km. north of this pass Newnham Col provides a possible route to the Cantabrae, although the complete crossing has not yet been made. The Dalmore Glacier is probably the biggest and most interest-ing of the Roslin's tributaries.

The Bjørnbo Gletscher is the last of the big glaciers

17

which drain into the Schuchert Dal and it equals the Roslin for length. Unlike the Roslin, however, it has many large and important tributaries. At Concordia, 15km. up the glacier, the Mars and Jupiter glaciers join the Bjørnbo which above this point is known as Main Glacier. The Jupiter in particular is a huge glacier in its own right, and is joined by the Orion Glacier to form a very complex system. At the head of Main Glacier easy cols give access to the Spörre and Borgbjerg glaciers. Downstream of Concordia the Bjørnbo is joined by the Saturn and Mercury glaciers to make it altogether the most extensive and complex glacier system in the Staunings Alps.

South-west of the Bjørnbo there are several smaller glacier systems; further west is the large Borgbjerg Gletscher, which can be regarded as forming the south-western boundary of the Staunings Alps. The Borgbjerg has its source in the same high snowfields as the Spörre and Main glaciers, and flows southwards towards Nordvest Fjord. The south-west corner of the Staunings Alps is the least explored part of the range.

Turning now to the principal mountains and their characteristics, we will return to the centre of the Staunings Alps where the Dansketinde, Hjornespids and Norsketinde (in that order) are the three highest and arguably the three finest peaks of the Staunings. All three are magnificently elegant granite peaks with narrow ridges and steep faces seamed by gullies. They are the equal of all but a few of the European mountains; they may lack the massive bulk of Mont Blanc and the sheer height of its Brenva Face but they can well be compared with the Aiguille Verte or the Schreckhorn.

North of this trio the Frihedstinde is the dominant mountain, not so much for its height as for its isolation in a part of the Staunings where few if any other peaks are outstanding. From the east and north-east the Frihedstinde appears as an isolated rocky pillar crowned with a cap of snow, and it is surprising that only one ascent has been made of this grand mountain.

The head of the Bersaerkerbrae is surrounded by some spectacular mountains, most of them 2400 to 2600m. high. As one approaches up the glacier the Bersaerkertinde dominates the view, with its 1500m. north face dropping in a single plunge from the level summit crest to the snows of the Bersaerkerbrae. This is one of the most spectacular sights in the Staunings Alps. East and north-east of the Bersaerkertinde the main peaks – Royal Peak, Kishmul and Glamis – gradually decrease in height towards Glamis Col, beyond which the character of the mountains diminishes. North-west of the Bersaerkertinde the mountain crest curves round towards Col Major over the flat-topped Merchiston and the fine twin peaks of the Knoxtinde (the original name given to this mountain, Grandes Jorasses, was doubtless inspired by the resemblance to the French mountain of the same name). On the Bersaerkerbrae side all these mountains are particularly impressive, being mainly steep ice faces and hanging glaciers.

The head of the Gully Gletscher is dominated by Bolvaerket, a remarkable rock peak rising like a huge wedge from the upper snowfields of the glacier. South of the Gully Gletscher, the area between it and the Sefstroms is a complex maze of peaks dominated by Korsspids and the Sefstromstinde, both mountains about 2700m. high. This is an area of sharp granite peaks, many of them comparable with the Chamonix aiguilles.

The head of the Sefstroms Glacier is surrounded by a host of grand mountains, including half a dozen of about 2700m. Of these, Snetoppen is the highest; it is a massive snow-capped mountain at the head of the Cantabrae. North of Snetoppen is Trinity, and south-east is Cantabrigia; both are magnificent steep rock peaks with no easy routes to their summits. North-west of Trinity a high and jagged ridge runs out to Attilaborgen and, beyond it, to the lower rock peaks above Dammen. Attilaborgen is a most impressive mountain, particularly as seen from the head of Dammen from where it appears as a huge blade of rock.

Elsewhere around the Sefstroms Glacier there are many

grand mountains ranging from the rock spires of Tantallon to the graceful snow ridges of Diadem and Downingfjeld. At the head of the glacier, Sefstromsgipfel is a lone mountain of more than 2700m.; beyond it, to the east, there are few outstanding mountains among the many dozens surrounding the Lang and Schuchert glaciers.

In the South and West Staunings there are few really outstanding mountains in the sense of height, isolation or appearance, although many of them are very hard to climb. In this area the mountain character is more homogeneous, yet it is still possible to select certain areas with particular features. The head of the Spörre Gletscher is a high-level snowfield surrounded by some fairly easy snow peaks, and so this area is a paradise for the ski-mountaineer. West of this the mountains between the Spörre and Prinsesse glaciers are more formidable, rising as they do very steeply from their glaciers. This is particularly true of the mountains round the Prinsesse Gletscher.

In the south there are dozens of fine mountains round the Roslin and Bjørnbo glaciers and some of them (for example the group south of Concordia on the Bjørnbo) offer excellent rock-climbing on their north faces, with easier routes on their south sides. It is generally true to say, however, that these mountains present less serious mountaineering problems than the big peaks of the Central Staunings.

Finally, in the south-west there is a fairly high and as yet unclimbed group near the head of the Borgbjerg Gletscher. The mountains in this area have a Cairngorm-like appearance with steep flanks and flat snow covered summits. They are in fact midway in character as well as position between the steep peaks of the Central Staunings and the vast flatness of the inland ice.

Approaches

The existence of the pack-ice drifting along the East Greenland coast during July and August makes it more or less impossible to be able to rely on sailing in to Mesters Vig within a given time. Delays of many days, or even weeks, are quite usual. For this reason all climbing parties going to Mesters Vig go by air. It may be possible to reduce air freight costs by sending heavy equipment by sea the previous year, but there is even an element of risk in doing this.

The usual approach to Mesters Vig is by the normal service flight from Europe to Reykjavik or Keflavik in Iceland, and from Reykjavik onwards by charter flight. Icelandair and one or two private operators now have considerable experience of the Reykjavik to Mesters Vig flight and can provide a variety of aircraft depending on the size of the party and the required payload.

At the time of writing (1971) it is necessary to obtain the permission of the Danish Civil Aviation Authority to fly to Mesters Vig, and to do so a party must be able to establish its bonafides and give assurance of adequate insurance to cover accidents and the possibility of emergency rescue flights.

At Mesters Vig visiting climbers should not count on being able to get supplies of any sort, either food or fuel, unless prior arrangements with the Station Manager have been made. (See later section on equipment.) Irregular postal services exist between Mesters Vig and the outside world, so mail can be sent out and received, depending on the frequency of flights. In an emergency it is possible to send out messages by radio. Camping is usually allowed near the airstrip, and there is a small timber hut that may be available for small parties.

Once at Mesters Vig there is a choice of approach routes to the mountains, but the decision depends to a large extent on the part of the mountains to which one is going. Parties heading for the eastern side of the Staunings Alps must walk in from Mesters Vig; parties heading for the west side of the range have a choice of walking through the mountains, walking round the coast by Kap Petersen, or taking a boat round Kap Petersen and up Alpe Fjord.

It has been possible in the past (but there is no certainty that it will always be possible) to hire a helicopter belonging to the Nordisk Mineselskab, which is usually based at Mesters Vig, to carry food and equipment into the mountains, but the payload of the helicopter is only about 300kg. and the cost of hire is considerable. The Station Manager at Mesters Vig has a motor launch which is also occasionally available for taking parties from Mesters Vig to Kap Petersen and Alpe Fjord.

The approach to the north-east corner of the Staunings Alps (Skeldal, Bersaerkerbrae) is short. From Mesters Vig a dusty 10km. road leads up the Tunnelelv to the old mine. Just beyond the mine two rivers converge, and the right-hand one (looking up the valley) is followed easily over heath and tundra for a further 6km. to the Gefion Pass (ca. 500m.). The pass gives the first view of the Staunings Alps proper, and a wonderful panorama it is, although the highest peaks are still hidden behind the lower hills on the opposite side of the Skeldal. The descent from the pass is easy, and the banks of the Skel river are soon reached.

There are fairly good camp-sites in the Skeldal between the Skel Glacier and the Bersaerkerbrae. The bottom of the valley is sandy and gravelly, the haunt of ringed plovers and the breeding ground of mosquitoes; better camp-sites can be found a few hundred metres up the hillsides where heath and tundra give more comfort.

For climbers heading for the Bersaerkerbrae the next problem is to cross the Skel river, which drains a large area of glacier and mountains and can at certain times of the day, and particularly in July, present some difficulty. Immediately below the Gefion Pass the river rushes through a gorge at the snout of the Bersaerkerbrae's terminal moraine, but upstream of this point it flows over gravel flats and is usually divided into two or three channels, making crossing easier. If a crossing of the river is not possible it is necessary to go about 3 km. upstream, cross the snout of the Skel Glacier, and so reach the west side of the river. This is a very rough journey, not to be measured in distance alone.

The best route up the Bersaerkerbrae starts on the south side of the huge terminal moraine and follows the little valley formed by the Bersaerkerbrae's southern lateral moraine. This has become something of a trade route and several cairns indicate the way along the moraine and eventually, after about 2½km., on to the ice of the glacier itself.

The Skel Glacier is about 13km. long and gives easy going with few crevasses. At its head the Skel Pass, easy on both sides, leads over to the Schuchert Gletscher and an easy descent to Malmberg. The Gefion and Skel passes give an easy route from Mesters Vig to the Schuchert Dal and the eastern and south-eastern glaciers of the Staunings.

An alternative route from Mesters Vig to the Schuchert Dal goes through the Werner Bjerge and over the Mellem Pass. From the old mine in the Tunnelelv the left hand (southerly) river is followed to an easy pass (vehicle tracks across the tundra show the way). Descending from this pass in a south-easterly direction one drops down towards the head of a large sea inlet called Mesters Vig (16km. south of the airstrip of the same name). Two streams must be crossed to reach the south side of the valley; then one comes to the hut at Sortjehorn standing prominently on a broad ridge 100–200m. above sea level. An alternative route to Sortjehorn from Mesters Vig is to go south-east along the edge of the inlet called Noret to the Hamma Hut, and then to follow the north-west shore of Mesters Vig inlet.

From Sortjehorn there is a grand view southwards up the Deltadal to the Werner Bjerge, with the rock peak Kolossen dividing the Mellem Gletscher on the right (west) from the Ostre Gletscher on the left (east). Bellevue is the graceful snow peak at the head of the Mellem Gletscher. The route from Sortjehorn contours above the bottom of the Deltadal (more vehicle tracks) and reaches the snout of the Mellem Gletscher which it ascends for about 8km. to the easy Mellem Pass. From this pass the Arcturus Glacier leads easily down to the ruined camp at Malmberg and the vast expanse of the Schuchert Gletscher (keep to the right of the Arcturus Glacier near its lower end).

South of Malmberg the Schuchert Gletscher becomes very rough as the relatively smooth icy surface gives way to the scree and boulders of the terminal moraine. The east side of the Schuchert Dal gives easier walking than the west side; however, the river emerging from the snout of the Schuchert Gletscher is very difficult if not impossible to cross, and for this reason climbers heading for the Staunings Alps must cross the glacier to the west of the valley and continue southwards along that side. The best crossing is opposite Malmberg, above the terminal moraine of the glacier which should be avoided as far as possible as it is a wilderness of boulders.

The journey round Kap Petersen and up to the head of Alpe Fjord is magnificent, either by boat or on foot. Every one of the 120km. is full of interest and beauty and the head of Alpe Fjord, where huge glaciers plunge into the water, is surrounded by towering mountains and is one of the grandest places imaginable. The walk is not always easy as there are one or two places where turbulent streams and very steep hillsides have to be crossed. A boat is essential for carrying food and equipment; it is quite usual for parties to use an inflatable rubber dinghy with outboard motor for this purpose while they themselves walk. In this way the journey to Alpe Fjord can be made in four or five days. More affluent parties may be able to afford large and powerful boats to carry themselves as well as their equipment, and so reduce the time for the journey to ten or twelve hours.

The journey by boat is not always simple for two principal hazards – wind and ice – may be encountered. The most likely wind hazard is the katabatic wind which, coming down from the ice-cap in the afternoons, blows very strongly along narrow, enclosed fiords like Alpe Fjord, whipping up quite stormy seas and making rubber dinghies, with their small freeboard, unseaworthy. Winds from the east are also troublesome as they blow the pack-ice onshore and make a boat journey along the coast difficult or impossible.

The second hazard is drifting ice – everything from large masses of pack-ice drifting through Kong Oscars Fjord to small pieces of brash ice which are often hard to spot in the water but whose sharp edges can tear open the hull of a rubber dinghy. The pack-ice moves with the wind, and changes of wind can completely alter the ice situation in an hour or two.

Generally speaking, during unsettled weather the calmest times are at night and one should be prepared to set off whenever the wind drops and the tide is favourable.

From Mesters Vig an easy walk leads north-westwards across tundra to the sandy shoreline of Kong Oscars Fjord, which is followed past a tiny hunters' hut to the Skel river. This crossing is the first obstacle, whose difficulty depends on the season of the year and the time of day. It may be necessary to use a boat to cross the shallow, sandy outflow of the river. Beyond the Skel the walk continues to be de-lightful and easy, with the spires of the Syltoppen on the left, and the Menanders Islands with their colonies of terns on the right. Beyond the outflow from the Skjoldungebrae (north-east branch) one reaches the hunters' hut at Kap Pet-ersen. This superbly situated hut, until recently used by hunters, has now become a stopping point for climbers en route to Alpe Fjord; however, it must be emphasised that the stores of food in the hut should not be used by visiting climbers. These stores are provided for hunters who may use the hut (possibly in an emergency) in winter.

The northern tip of Scoresby Land just beyond Kap Pet-ersen is rocky and inhospitable, with steep cliffs and scree dropping into the fiord. The usual walking route is up the north-eastern outflow of the Skjoldungebrae and down the north-western outflow and the Skipperdal to reach Alpe Fjord west of Kap Petersen. The route up and down the glacier is easy although the terminal moraines are rough. South-westwards along the shore of the fiord, the going is easy for several km. until past the outflow of the Linne and Sedgwick glaciers; then the fiord becomes progressively narrower and more deeply enclosed by mountains. On the north side the 1500m. high Berzelius Bjerge rises in steep walls of multi-coloured rock in a single sweep from water's edge to snowy crest.

Beyond the Sedgwick Gletscher one has to climb over a rocky buttress and traverse scree before descending again to the flat land at the outflow of the Fangshytte Gletscher. On the south side of the outflow there is a small hunters' hut in a very poor state of repair.

The next 8km. to the Vikingebrae is the hardest part of the walk. Gradually the hillside becomes steeper, with huge scree slopes and rock buttresses dropping sheer into the water. The climber has sometimes to climb above the buttresses and traverse unstable scree, and sometimes to traverse the buttresses themselves with the icy waters of Alpe Fjord below his heels. Eventually the going becomes easier and one drops to pleasant tundra at the outflow of the Vikingebrae, where there are good camp sites.

Now at last the climber feels that he is nearing his goal. The head of Alpe Fjord is only 15km. ahead beyond the ice-barrier formed by the snout of the Gully and Sefstroms glaciers, and the mountains of the Staunings Alps on the east side of the fiord begin to show their real character. In particular, the Norsketinde dominates the view up the Vikingebrae and it is no wonder that this magnificent rock and ice peak was one of the first of the Staunings to attract the early climbers. By contrast the mountains of Nathorsts Land on the west side of the fiord are lower and less formidable. The Schaffhauserdal (opposite the Vikingebrae) is a broad, open valley which leads up to the ice-cap and a range of more modest peaks.

Six km. beyond the Vikingebrae one comes to the Gully Gletscher and good camp sites near its lateral moraine. The Gully and Sefstroms glaciers converge just above the edge of the fiord and their combined snout, a huge fan of contorted ice 5km. wide, juts out into Alpe Fjord and almost reaches its western shore. A channel 5km. long and in places only a few hundred metres wide leads from the main fiord into the inner fiord called Dammen. The passage by boat of this channel with the ice cliffs of the glacier on one hand, the rock cliffs of Nathorsts Land on the other, and small icebergs drifting between, is the highlight of the journey to the head of Alpe Fjord. At times, depending on the wind, the channel may be blocked by drifting pack-ice; at other times it may be quite clear. Beware of huge seracs collapsing off the snout of the glacier and creating a tidal wave in the narrow waters.

Dammen, the innermost sanctuary of Alpe Fjord, is reminiscent of Loch Coruisk on a grand scale. It is 5km. long and completely enclosed by mountains and glaciers. Here the climber feels completely isolated in his own world of infinite peace and grandeur. The silence of the arctic is broken only occasionally by the lapping of water on the rocky shore, the crack and rumble of falling ice and the haunting cry of the great northern diver echoing among the crags.

Possible landing places and camp sites exist on the east shore (either near the lateral moraine of the Sefstroms Glacier, or a kilometre or two further on) and at the head of Dammen where the terminal moraine of the Spörre Gletscher is flat and sandy near the water's edge. Two factors must be borne in mind when selecting a camp site. The first is the availability of water which may be a problem, and the second is the katabatic wind which can blow very strongly across the unsheltered shores of Dammen. There is also a good camp site about 250m. above sea level at a little lake nestling on the south-west side of the Sefstroms' lateral moraine.

West of Dammen the terminal moraine of the Spörre Gletscher fills the valley for 5km. with its debris of boulders and gravel, and beyond this is the lake called Furesö, 20km. long and so deeply enclosed by mountains as to seem perpetually dark and gloomy.

Mountaineering

Despite their quite modest height, the Staunings Alps have all the characteristics of mountains twice as high in other parts of the world, and they can be compared with the European Alps to which they are similar in scale and appearance. Rising as they do from sea level or from glaciers only 300–600m. above sea level, the Staunings Alps often give more actual climbing then the European Alps. For example there is a lot more climbing in the ascent of the Sefstromstinde (2800m.) from the head of Alpe Fjord than in the ascent of the Matterhorn from Zermatt.

The mountains are well covered with snow and ice, and many huge glaciers radiate from the heart of the range towards the surrounding fiords and valleys. Generally the north faces are snow and ice covered, and the south faces are rocky. As far as the glaciers are concerned, the Staunings are more than equal to the European Alps; only the Aletschgletscher in Switzerland is comparable in length with the big Staunings glaciers.

For all practical purposes the climbing season in the Staunings Alps lasts for two months – July and August. Earlier in the year there is too much snow on the mountains, and in June conditions of warm weather and continuous melting give almost impossible walking conditions on the glaciers, and skis are essential. It would be possible to travel and climb in other parts of Scoresby Land earlier in the year; for example, ski-mountaineering over the smooth glaciers of the Werner Bjerge in May or June would probably be an attractive proposition.

The Greenland summer is short and by the end of August the first frosts and snowfalls of autumn are likely. The temperature, particularly in the mountains, drops sharply and early snowfalls remain unmelted on the peaks. There is, however, a wonderful quality to the late August and early

September days with their clear, cold air and the glowing autumn colours in the tundra and along the fiord shores.

Of the two months that make the short climbing season, August is generally considered to be the better. In July the summer thaw is still likely to be in progress and the glaciers are still covered with soft snow. The night temperatures at glacier level are not low enough to freeze the snow, which is generally rather soft and slushy. In these conditions long approach marches up glaciers are likely to be very arduous. In August, however, the snow becomes fairly well consolidated and the onset of night frosts at about this time produce a further improvement on the glaciers, especially in the early hours of the day. Towards the end of August, just before the first autumn snows, the conditions probably reach their best with firm, well frozen snow throughout the day.

The northern part of Scoresby Land has a reputation for fine weather in summer and this reputation is probably well-deserved. Not for nothing is the area known as the Arctic Riviera. The climber can therefore be reasonably confident of good weather, and winds are in general light in the mountains. (Paradoxically the winds at sea level are often much stronger.) These factors, combined with twenty-four hours of daylight per day in July and August, make for ideal climbing conditions in which the climber can never be benighted, and can go on climbing for as long as he has strength and energy.

Mid-day temperatures in July are often uncomfortably warm for climbing and load-carrying. In such weather it is more pleasant to travel and climb by night when the heat and glare of mid-day is replaced by a wonderfully cool clarity as the sun drops towards the northern horizon.

The snow and ice climbing of the Staunings Alps is of a very high quality. Climbing conditions on the mountain are usually good in July and August, and may be rather easier in the former month. Generally in July the gullies are well filled with snow which, provided it is not too soft, makes for rapid and easy climbing. In August the gullies may become very icy and correspondingly harder. Some of the peaks are

characterised by forbiddingly steep ice slopes which would give ice climbing of a very high standard, but few routes of this nature have yet been attempted.

The quality of the rock is very variable, not only from one part of the range to another, but also on different parts of a single mountain. At its best the rock is excellent granite, and this rock predominates in the centre of the range on the highest peaks. Elsewhere the rock is of more doubtful quality and in some places is thoroughly bad. Fortunately the bad areas are in general on the northern and eastern perimeter of the Staunings where the peaks are lower and of less interest. Everywhere the climber must remember that he is climbing rock that at most has been climbed only once or twice before and is being constantly subjected to the action of frost and thaw; so the greatest care in testing holds is necessary at all times.

Glacier travel and route finding provide some of the greatest interest that the Staunings have to offer. Although most of the main glaciers are easy, the subsidiary glaciers by which the high peaks are approached are often steep and broken by big icefalls. Many of these glaciers call for mountaineering and route finding ability of a high order. There are several excellent routes through the mountains which cross passes and glaciers and although they may not include any summits, they are nevertheless full of mountaineering interest.

Objective dangers in the mountains cannot be ignored. Snow and ice avalanches are not particularly common but rock falls are quite common in the latter part of the summer as the snow melts off rocky ridges, walls and gullies. A gully which in July might give a quick and easy route can in August become a death-trap of falling stones; however, the danger is usually fairly obvious and may be avoided by climbing at night or early in the morning.

There is one hazard in the Staunings that is not often met in the European mountains – namely streams of meltwater on the lower glaciers. Particularly during July, when the melting is at its height, considerable streams of meltwater develop on the glacier surfaces and rush down until they disappear into moulins. Some of these streams carve wide and deep channels across the glacier surface and may be awkward to cross. Great care should be taken in crossing these streams for their sides are very slippery, and a fall into such a stream could well have disastrous consequences as the climber would be carried away at a great rate with little chance of saving himself.

To sum up, the Staunings Alps offer the climber probably the best mountaineering in Greenland, with a great variety of climbing and mountain travel. There is scope for climbs of all standards; however, it should be emphasised that the Staunings must be treated with the greatest of respect. They are mountains for competent climbers, and in particular for climbers with experience of big glaciated mountains and with the ability to find routes where no other climbers have been before.

History of the Exploration

The earliest exploration of the coast of North-East Greenland dates back to the first half of the last century when many expeditions, some of them British, made short summer visits and named many of the principal parts of the coast-land. Scoresby Land, for example, is named after the Scottish whaling captain William Scoresby. Towards the end of the last century more ambitious expeditions wintered in North-East Greenland and brought back the first reports of snow, ice and climatic conditions in winter.

In 1927 the Danes resettled about a hundred Eskimos from Angmagssalik to Scoresbysund and thereby established the most northerly Eskimo settlement in East Greenland.

In the nineteen thirties there was intense activity along the coast from Scoresby Sound northwards for about 600km. to Danmarks Havn as both Denmark and Norway tried to establish sovereignty over this part of Greenland. Eventually a decision of the International Court in 1933 acknowledged Greenland to be Danish territory.

The pre-war activity and exploration in North-East Greenland was based at stations on Ella Island and Clavering Island (both north of Scoresby Land), and expeditions were led by Dr. Lauge Koch and the American Miss Louise Boyd. Scientific work was started, wireless and weather reporting stations were established, and hunters from Norway and Denmark roamed up and down the coast driving their dogs and sledges in search of polar bears and arctic foxes.

During the war a strange conflict occurred between a party of Germans who established a weather reporting station on Sabine Island (74½°N) and the North-East Greenland Sledge Patrol. The Sledge Patrol, a dozen strong, was composed of Danish, Norwegian and Eskimo hunters who were left behind in North-East Greenland at the beginning of the war, and were themselves transmitting weather reports to Britain and America. For two months in the spring of 1943 the two groups stalked each other through the frozen fiords, and for the first and only time in Greenland men hunted each other. However, as the fiord ice melted in the early summer of that year the Germans departed and peace returned to the arctic. The whole story is vividly told in David Howarth's book *The Sledge Patrol.*

After the war geological research was resumed, and in 1948 lead was discovered. Exploration became intense and the discovery of rich deposits of lead and zinc ores in northern Scoresby Land led to the establishment of the mine, airstrip and harbour at Mesters Vig. From that time onwards regular scientific expeditions were carried out in North-East Greenland under the leadership of Dr. Lauge Koch. The entire coastal strip, fiords and islands between Scoresby Land (71°N) and Hochstetter's Forland (76°N) have now been thoroughly explored.

The first mountain exploration in the Werner Bjerge and the Staunings Alps was carried out by geologists of Nordisk Mineselskab and members of Lauge Koch's expeditions in the early nineteen fifties. However, several years were to elapse before the first of the large mountaineering expeditions went to Mesters Vig and the Staunings Alps.

1950

In 1950 the Swiss geologist Gerold Styger climbed a fine peak of nearly 1800m. on the Skel–Schuchert watershed two km. north-west of the Skel Pass. This may well have been the first major climb in the Staunings Alps, and the peak has become known as *Swiss Peak.* The ascent was almost certainly made from the south by a side glacier of the Schuchert which leads to a pass a short distance south-west of the summit.

In the same year the Swiss, Peter Braun and Fritz Schwartzenbach, visited the Vikingebrae and climbed the *Kathispids* (1890m.).

1951

In the following year they returned to the Skjoldungebrae and climbed the *Solvhorn* (1850m.) from a camp near the foot of the glacier. The climb up the snow covered north side of the mountain was made on skis. Then Braun and Schwartzenbach moved on to the head of the Skjoldungebrae and climbed the *Frihedstinde* (2610m.) by a gully on the north face overlooking the Friheds Pass, and the *Elizabethstinde* (2250m.) on the opposite side of the Skjoldungebrae.

The second ascent of the Elizabethtinde was made a week or two later by the Norwegian climbers A. R. Heen, K. Barstad and O. Roed who left their camp at Kap Petersen a few hours before the return of the previous party, and did not know of the first ascent. The Norwegians also climbed *Tarnfjeld* and *Vardefjeld*, two peaks on the east side of the Skjoldungebrae about 10km. north-east of the Elizabethtinde.

1954

In 1954 Heen, Roed and the Danes E. Jensen and E. Hoff established their base camp at the foot of the Vikingebrae. From a higher camp on the Invertebrae they climbed the *Norsketinde* (2860m.) by an ice gully leading to the north-west ridge of the peak. This party also made a reconnaissance as far as the Helvedes Pass at the head of the Vikingebrae, and climbed the two peaks of about 1900m. which overlook Alpe Fjord from either side of the foot of the glacier.

In the same summer a geological party from Dr Lauge Koch's expedition made an extensive aerial reconnaissance and survey of the Staunings Alps. The leader of this party was the Swiss scientist John Haller and he was accompanied by Wolfgang Diehl and Schwartzenbach. After the flight they established their base camp near Dammen at the head of Alpe Fjord. They ascended the Gully Gletscher, solving for the first time the problems posed by the three great ice-falls, and from a camp in the upper basin of the glacier they climbed the *Dansketinde* (2930m.) from the south-east. Returning to Dammen, they then explored the Sefstroms Glacier, penetrating about 25km. up the glacier on skis but being prevented by unfavourable weather from doing any climbs. Finally Diehl and Schwartzenbach made the second ascent of the Norsketinde by the original route.

1957

In 1957 the first large expedition went to the Staunings Alps. A party of eight climbers, mostly Austrians led by Hans Gsellmann, flew directly to Dammen in a Catalina flying boat and were thus able to establish themselves very early in the season, before the pack-ice would have permitted an approach by sea.

Their first exploration took them to the Furesö; some members canoed to the head of this bleak lake and ascended the Violin Gletscher for a short distance towards the inland ice. The *Eckhorn*, an angular peak at the south-east corner of the Furesö, was also climbed.

The Austrians then went up the Sefstroms Glacier and camped at the foot of the Kirkbrae. From there they climbed about ten mountains, all first ascents, using skis for many of the long glacier approaches.

Near their camp the Austrians climbed the *Sefstroms-tinde* by its south ridge, a 1800m. climb direct from glacier to summit. At the head of the Sefstroms Glacier another peak over 2700m., the *Sefstromsgipfel*, was climbed, probably by way of the col at the head of the glacier. The Grantabrae was ascended and at its head three snow peaks, the *Diadem*, were climbed.

Other Austrian climbs included *Bavariaspids* at the head of the Kirkbrae, *Dreikant* on the south side of this glacier, *Kapelle* and *Mitterspids* on the north side, and *Kastenberg* on the south-west of the Sefstroms Glacier. Two other peaks mentioned in the Austrians' report are *Sonnblickspids* and *Weisse Wand*. The exact position of these mountains is not clear from their map, although the latter seems to be very close to the Korsspids. The topography of the mountains between the Gully and Sefstroms glaciers is rather complicated.

At the end of their expedition the Austrians hoped to return from the Sefstroms Glacier to Mesters Vig by the Lang Gletscher; however, they were unsuccessful in this. Probably they were deterred by the prospect of getting their loaded sledge over the col separating the Grantabrae from the Lang Glacier; so they returned to Alpe Fjord. Gsellmann then canoed back to Mesters Vig and was fortunate to find Knut Lauritzen, the Danish shipping magnate, holidaying in the area in his yacht the 'Netta Dan'. Lauritzen sailed to Alpe Fjord and brought out the stranded Austrians.

1958
Early in July 1958 the Scottish East Greenland Expedition, led by Malcom Slesser, arrived at Mesters Vig and set up its first base camp in the Skeldal, a kilometre or so below the snout of the Skel Glacier. It was an exceptionally hot and sunny month, the snow on the glaciers was very soft and the Skel river was difficult to cross. The Kishmul Glacier, the biggest tributary of the Skel Glacier, was explored and an easy pass, Glamis Col, was crossed to reach the Bersaerkerbrae. Three peaks were climbed from the Skeldal camp – Swiss Peak by its north ridge from the Skel Glacier, *Glamis* (the first big mountain south-west of Glamis Col) from the Kishmul Glacier, and *Dunvegan* (the highest and most prominent rock peak on the Skel-Bersaerkerbrae divide) directly from the Skeldal.

A higher camp was made just below the junction of the Dunottar Glacier with the Bersaerkerbrae. (This camp, called Sun Valley Camp, has become one of the most popular camp-sites in the Staunings Alps, with level platforms for at least twelve tents on the lateral moraine and a good water supply.) The Bersaerkerbrae approaches to Col Major were explored for the first time and Kenneth Bryan and Donald Bennet made the first ascent of the east side of the col. The big gully appeared at that time to be very steep and icy, and the rock buttress immediately to its north was climbed. However, this route has not much to recommend itself and has never been repeated, the gully being now the standard route on the Bersaerkerbrae side of the col.

Four mountains were climbed from the Sun Valley Camp. Three of them were at the head of the Dunottar Glacier, and included *Dunottar* itself, a fine 2500m. peak approached by the easy snow slopes of its north side. The fourth peak climbed was *Merchistontinde*, the flat-topped mountain which is prominent in the view up the lower reaches of the Bersaerkerbrae on the right (north-west) of the Bersaerkertinde.

Late in July, as the ice in Kong Oscars Fjord broke up, the expedition moved on foot and by small boat round the coast to Alpe Fjord and camped by the water's edge at Dammen. The Sefstroms Glacier was the main centre of activity. From a camp at the foot of the Sefstromstinde's south ridge three peaks were climbed to the east and south-east of this, the dominant mountain of the area. *Ruthven* was climbed by the long snow gully between it and the Sefstromstinde (on this occasion the gully was well filled with snow, at other times it may be very icy and a chute for falling stones), *Tantallon* was climbed up the steep little glacier on the south-east of the Sefstromstinde, and *Beaufort* (the rock spire next to Kapelle) was climbed directly from this glacier. The *Sefstromstinde* and *Attilaborgen* were unsuccessfully attempted although on the latter Slesser and Douglas Scott were turned back only a couple of hundred metres below the top, more by exhaustion than by technical difficulty, after a very long climb.

Finally the expedition divided into three groups. Slesser and Iain Smart made the long crossing from Alpe Fjord to Syd Kap at the mouth of Nordvest Fjord and back by the Spörre and Roslin glaciers, climbing *Roslinborg* on the way.

Bryan and Leonard Lovat climbed the four rock peaks between Dammen and the lower Sefstroms Glacier, of which the twin-topped *Inverarnan* is the highest. The third group crossed to Nathorsts Land and reached the ice-cap by the Sydvest Gletscher (Map 2).

At the end of August the party returned to Mesters Vig. Slesser, Bryan and Charles Rose made the traverse by the Gully Gletscher, Col Major and the Bersaerkerbrae, while the others returned by boat.

The most important item of scientific work done by the expedition was a glaciological survey of the lower Sefstroms Glacier carried out under the direction of Stanley Paterson.

1960

In July 1960 a second British expedition arrived at Mesters Vig. The thirty or so members of this expedition included about ten experienced climbers from the Scottish Mountaineering Club and the Alpine Club, and twenty boys having their first taste of exploratory mountaineering. The leader was John Hunt.

For once the weather of the Arctic Riviera turned out bad, and a combination of very late melting snow and frequent rain storms produced difficult conditions for travelling and left the high peaks heavily plastered with snow.

In late July the climbers pushed laboriously up the Bersaerkerbrae. From a camp low down on the glacier two peaks were climbed at the head of a side glacier named the Caerleon Glacier. On a third peak a party of four had a narrow escape when a cornice broke away under the expedition leader; however, Alan Blackshaw saved the day in textbook style by leaping in the opposite direction. The climb was abandoned. (Thinking they were on a virgin peak the party, despite their failure, christened this mountain *Caerleon*. However, recent maps show this mountain as *Tarnfjeld*, climbed by the Norwegians several years earlier. There is still some doubt about this point.)

Meanwhile Malcolm Slesser's party higher up the Ber-saerkerbrae climbed *Tintagel*, the peak overlooking the big bend in the glacier. Then Slesser and Ian McNaught-Davis climbed the *Bersaerkerspire*, a magnificent blade of granite, by the slabs and chimneys of its south face; an excellent rock climb. Two more peaks on the east side of the Ber-saerkerbrae were climbed before the entire expedition started to move on to Alpe Fjord.

Slesser, McNaught-Davis, Hunt and John Jackson crossed Col Major and from a camp at the head of the Gully Glets-cher the first two climbed the *Hjornespids* by its south-east ridge. This was a magnificent climb over a long and difficult ridge, bristling with gendarmes, and it was certainly the most difficult climb undertaken in the Staunings Alps up to that time. The descent was made by the south ridge and the total time for the climb was thirty hours.

At Alpe Fjord the expedition was beset by mishaps, and only after considerable delays were their food supplies at Mesters Vig transported to Alpe Fjord by boat, and to Schuchert Dal by air. Nevertheless two parties led by Hunt and George Lowe, made the Spörre–Duart–Roslin glaciers crossing and reached the lower Schuchert Dal. After spend-ing two days searching for their food supplies (which were due to arrive by air) Hunt's party went up the Bjørnbo Gletscher to the great confluence of glaciers which they named Concordia. In the last three days Hunt, Blackshaw and some of the boys climbed four mountains and explored two of the tributaries of the Bjørnbo – the Mercury and Jupiter glaciers. This was the first exploration of the South Staunings, and it revealed a vast area of huge glaciers and unclimbed mountains.

During the last two weeks at Alpe Fjord all climbing efforts were frustrated by the bad weather which also pre-vented the motor boat *Polypen* from bringing in food and climbers. John Sugden, however, continued the glaciological survey work on the Sefstroms Glacier that had been started by Paterson two years earlier.

1961

Sir John Hunt's report of his brief visit to the South Staunings at the end of the 1960 expedition inspired Jim Clarkson the following year to organise a full-scale expedition to that area. The nine members of his party were all members of the Junior Mountaineering Club of Scotland.

Arriving at Mesters Vig early in July, they set off on foot over the Gefion and Skel passes towards the Bjørnbo Gletscher and a promised air-drop of food and equipment at Concordia. Heavily laden, they took seven days to reach the Bjørnbo, finding on the way considerable difficulty in crossing the river flowing from the Lang Gletscher.

Once at Concordia, with food for four weeks, the expedition enjoyed a feast of first ascents. In the first week, climbing from Concordia, five rock peaks were climbed including *Sentinel*, the very prominent mountain between the Pegasus and Main glaciers.

In the next ten days a party of four led by Howard Brunton set out on skis to attempt the crossing to the head of Alpe Fjord, 50km. north of Concordia. An easy col was crossed at the head of the Main Glacier, and on the north side beautiful snow slopes led down easily to the ice-falls of the lower Spörre Gletscher. These presented considerable difficulties and two of the party had narrow escapes in crevasses. After five hard days the party reached Dammen and returned to Concordia by the same route.

Meanwhile the climbing party moved to the Mercury Glacier, south of Concordia. Five mountains were climbed, including the principal rock peak which was called *The Citadel*.

After the return of the Alpe Fjord party the entire expedition moved up the Jupiter Glacier to the highest and most difficult peaks of the South Staunings. In perfect conditions characteristic of August about twelve mountains were climbed. One party climbed *Prometheus*, between the Taurus and Orion glaciers, the highest peak of the South Staunings and about 2570m. high. The hardest climb was *Wedge Peak*, whose north face gave Keith Murray and

Michael Fleming a twelve hour climb of great difficulty.

This was a most successful expedition which climbed in all twenty-four virgin peaks. By contrast with the high mountains of the Central Staunings, the South Staunings were found to be relatively easy, and climbing times from glacier camps were (with notable exception of *Wedge Peak*) usually less than eight hours.

In the same summer an expedition of the Bangor Junior Mountaineering Club, from the University College of North Wales, led by M. K. Lyon, explored the Schuchert and Lang glaciers and the surrounding mountains. Flying in to Mesters Vig on the same flight as Clarkson's party, they took the same route to the Schuchert Gletscher and camped on the west side of the glacier opposite Malmberg. In the Schuchert Gletscher area the very fine *Royal Peak* on the north side of the glacier was climbed together with the neighbouring *Point Neurose*. Two smaller peaks on the south side of the glacier were also climbed.

The Lang Gletscher was explored and a short cut from the Schuchert to the Lang was discovered over a col due west of Malmberg which gave access to a tributary of the Lang. From an advanced base camp on the Lang Gletscher four peaks on the north-east side of the glacier, and *Santes Fair* on the south side, were climbed.

A small group pushed on to Crescent Col at the head of the Lang where Barry Brewster had a bad accident, falling down to the head of the Gully Gletscher. He was carried back to the advanced base camp while two members of the expedition made a rapid dash to Malmberg. By great good fortune an American helicopter at Mesters Vig was able to fly immediately to the Lang, and Brewster was quickly evacuated to Iceland.

1962 was a blank year in the Staunings Alps as the Danish Government refused permission to all parties that year. At that time, with the closing of the lead and zinc mine at Mesters Vig, air and sea traffic to this part of the world was decreasing considerably.

1963

This year saw a resurgence and two large expeditions from British universities were given permission to visit Scoresby Land. Both these expeditions were strongly supported by the Mount Everest Foundation, which may explain why the Danish Government regarded them favourably. The weather that summer was said to have been the worst recorded for many years, and it is remarkable that so much good climbing was done.

The Cambridge University East Greenland Expedition was led by Colin Knox and had twelve members. It was probably the most ambitious expedition ever to go to the Staunings Alps; a big air-drop of food and equipment was made on the Sefstroms Glacier. The activity of the expedition was centred in the Gully and Sefstroms glaciers but a good deal of far ranging exploration was done elsewhere. Scientific work included a continuation of the glaciological work of Paterson and Sugden on the Sefstroms Gletscher, a study of atmospheric radio noise, and a collection of geological specimens.

The advance party made the Bersaerkerbrae–Col Major–Gully Gletscher crossing in difficult conditions at the beginning of July to await the arrival of the air-drop on the Sefstroms Gletscher. By mid-July the rest of the expedition followed and reached base camp at the little lake above Dammen.

In the next five weeks a great many climbs were done. In the Cantabrae, at the head of the Sefstroms Glacier, *Trinity, Snetoppen, Pembroke* and *Cantabrigia* (all about 2800m.) were climbed, and Newnham Col was reached but not descended on its south side to the Roslin Gletscher. Lower down the Cantabrae, just above its junction with the Sefstroms, a long traverse of three peaks – *Sidney, Sussex* and *Emmanuel* – was made. On the south-east side of the Grantabrae the big snow mountain *Downingfield* was climbed (this may have been climbed by the Austrians in 1957 as one of the three peaks called Diadem). Lower down the Sefstroms Glacier *Attilaborgen* was climbed by the route attempted by the Scots in 1958.

In the Gully Gletscher three peaks on the north side of the glacier and five on the south side were climbed. The latter group was climbed from a high camp in the Cavendish Glacier, which drops in a huge icefall to meet the Gully between its second and third icefalls, and included the 2780m. *Korsspids*. (This was almost certainly the first ascent of the Korsspids as there was no sign of a previous visit by the Austrians). At the head of the Gully Gletscher, *Bolvaerket* and the *Grandes Jorasses* were climbed, the former being the hardest climb of the expedition and the only one to be rated TD on the Alpine grading system. (Grandes Jorasses appears to have been renamed by the Danish Geodetic Institute, and will probably appear on future maps either as the C. F. Knox Tinde or simply as Knoxtinde.)

The Krabbe Gletscher was visited and great difficulty was found in making any progress up this very broken little glacier. Eventually a route across the glacier and up its southwest flanking wall was found and *Queenstinde* was climbed; however, no possible pass at the head of the glacier was found.

In addition to this impressive list of climbs, several long traverses through the range were made and new passes crossed. Between the head of the Lang and the Kirkbrae the Churchill Col was discovered. A long traverse from the Gully Gletscher to Kong Oscars Fjord was made by the Vertebrae, Word e Pass, Invertebrae, Friheds Gletscher, Friheds Pass and the Skjoldungebrae. Another long traverse was made from the head of the Lang Gletscher to Mesters Vig by the Trumpington Col, Schuchert Glacier and the Skel Pass.

This expedition is undoubtedly the most successful to have visited the Staunings Alps to date when judged by its list of climbs, many of which were of length and difficulty comparable with the best classic Alpine routes.

The Imperial College (London) Expedition of the same

year was led by M. H. Key, and had eight members. The entire activity of this expedition was centred on the Bersaerkerbrae and its neighbouring glaciers, and was divided between climbing and glaciological surveying.

Conditions on the Bersaerkerbrae were very difficult when the expedition arrived in early July. Deep soft snow in a continuous state of melting made progress up the glacier very difficult, and the first week was spent on the lower peaks near the foot of the glacier. At the head of the Caerleon Glacier first ascents of two small rock peaks were made and *Tarnfjeld*, the peak on which John Hunt's party had nearly come to grief three years earlier, was also climbed. (This was claimed as a first ascent of Caerleon, but there is some doubt as to whether Tarnfjeld and Caerleon are the same peak or not.) In the Harlech Glacier five more rock peaks of about 1800m. were climbed.

In due course, as conditions improved, the expedition moved further up the glacier and in August several major climbs were done round the head of the Bersaerkerbrae. *Lambeth, Kensington, Notting Hill* and *Kishmul* (named but not climbed by the Scots in 1958) were all worthy first ascents, and second ascents were (unwittingly) made of *Merchistontinde, Grandes Jorasses* and *Royal Peak*. The ascent of Grandes Jorasses from the upper basin of the Bersaerkerbrae was a particularly fine climb: the hardest of the expedition and a harder route than the one taken by the Cambridge party from the Gully Gletscher two weeks earlier.

Finally *Richmond*, the highest of a not very distinguished group of rock peaks between the Kishmul Glacier and the Edinbrae, was climbed.

In the same year, 1963, the Italian climber Guido Monzino assembled a large party of his countrymen and marched up the Bersaerkerbrae. The sole achievement of this ambitious outing was the second ascent of Glamis by a new route from the Bersaerkerbrae.

1964

In the following year Monzino returned to the Staunings Alps with twenty companions and they sailed round to Alpe Fjord in a small fleet of rubber boats. On the south side of the Vikingebrae two very fine rock peaks, *Cima Est* and *Cima Ouest*, were climbed; both first ascents. The party then proceeded to the head of the Vikingebrae and made the second ascent of the *Dansketinde* by a new route up its snow covered north-east face.

In the same year, 1964, a Swiss expedition from the Academischer Alpen-Club Zürich visited the Staunings Alps. Following the usual pattern, the party of ten arrived at Mesters Vig in mid-July. In the next ten days they made five first ascents in the *Syltoppen range* overlooking Kong Oscars Fjord between Mesters Vig and Kap Petersen. These very impressive looking little mountains are unfortunately composed of very loose rock, amounting in places to scree lying at its angle of repose, and climbs tend to be dangerous rather than difficult.

Moving round to Alpe Fjord, the Swiss party camped at the foot of the Knacke Gletscher, the tributary of the Sefstroms Glacier on the north-west side of the Sefstromstinde. From there they made first ascents of four peaks bordering the Knacke Gletscher, and one peak, *Helmspitzen,* southwest of Kastenberg. (One of the peaks climbed at the head of the Knacke Gletscher, named *Weydmannsburg* by the Swiss, is marked on their map as being very close to the Korsspids and Weisse Wand, and there remains some doubt as to the exact relationship of these peaks.) The Swiss also made second ascents of *Tantallon*, by the Knacke Gletscher, and the *Sefstromstinde* by the 900m. gully between it and Ruthven.

Continuing to the head of Dammen, the Swiss party made several more first ascents. These included *Pyramid Peak,* the very prominent mountain at the south-west corner of Dammen, which dominates the view up to the head of Alpe Fjord. It was indeed surprising that this peak survived so long before being climbed. From a camp about 6 km. up the Spörre Gletscher, eight peaks were climbed on the east and west sides of the glacier; thus one of the last major unexplored areas of the Staunings Alps was opened up. In the next few years this area was due to receive considerable attention.

1966

In 1966 a German party under the leadership of Karl Herrligkoffer, of Nanga Parbat fame, flew out to Mesters Vig at the beginning of August. It had been their original intention to go on to Peary Land in the extreme north of Greenland; however, they were unable to obtain fuel supplies at Mesters Vig for their flight northwards and so they turned their attention to the Staunings Alps.

Fortunately they were able to borrow three boats at Mesters Vig and, with the help of the Danish Air Force who dropped their food supplies on the Spörre Gletscher, the party was able to establish itself within a week at a high camp at about 1600m. near the Duart–Roslin col.

From this camp during the last two weeks of August, the Germans made ascents of about thirty summits in the area at the head of the Spörre, Duart, Roslin, Main and Borgbjerg glaciers. This is an area of extensive high snowfields and the mountains are very much easier than those further north-east. Many of them are snowy domes, connected by high ridges, rising only one or two thousand feet from the glacier snowfields. The Germans made good use of skis (the upper basin of the Spörre Gletscher is ideal for ski-mountaineering) and in some very long days they were able to traverse three or four peaks in quick succession. On one particular day the ten man party climbed eleven peaks.

Although the Germans claimed all their climbs, except *Roslinborg*, as first ascents, it seems certain that three or four of them were in fact second ascents of peaks climbed by the Swiss two years earlier; they also almost certainly made the second ascent of *Darien*, the peak near the col crossed by members of the Scottish 1961 expedition on their route from Concordia to Dammen.

1967

In 1967 four more German climbers from Berchtesgaden – Sepp Kurz, Hermann Ponn, Hans Richter and Carl de Temple – went to the area west of the Spörre Gletscher. They ascended the Hecate Glacier and from a camp at about 1500m. they made first ascents of thirteen peaks. Most of these peaks were on the divide between the Prinsesse Gletscher and the Spörre, Castor and Hecate glaciers; the highest was *Schneekuppe*, a massive snow-capped mountain 2640m. high between the Spörre and Prinsesse glaciers. In addition the Germans climbed three peaks on the ridge separating the Castor and Pollux glaciers. (There seems to be some confusion about the names of these glaciers for the Castor, Pollux and Hecate glaciers appear in German climbing reports as the Grosse Sidney, Kleine Sidney and Berchtesgadener glaciers.)

In the same year the well-known Italian climber Toni Gobbi led a party of twelve to the Staunings Alps. They arrived in mid-June, much earlier than most expeditions, but they intended to use skis as much as possible on all their climbs. From a camp on the Bersaerkerbrae they made ascents of Col Major, Dunottar and Kensington (both second ascents) and Glamis (third ascent). They then crossed the Glamis Col to the Kishmul Glacier, making the first ascent of *Panoramic Peak* immediately to the north of the col.

1968

The following year, 1968, was one of the busiest ever in the Staunings Alps. In addition to two large university expeditions, several small groups of climbers from Europe shared a charter flight, and a large French expedition was also in the field.

The eight man Queen Mary College Expedition was led by Keith Miller. They flew in to Mesters Vig at the beginning of July and set up their base camp on the Bersaerkerbrae at Sun Valley Camp. The climbing activities of the expedition were centred on the Bersaerkerbrae, with an advanced camp on Col Major. The most important climbs done were the first ascent of the *Bersaerkertinde*, and the second ascent of the *Hjornespids* by a new route.

The Bersaerkertinde, which looks so impregnable from the north, was climbed by Malcolm Munro, Dick Palmer and Eric Williams in a three-day trip which took them over the top of *Merchiston* and along the ridge connecting it to the Bersaerkertinde. The return was made by the same route. Hjornespids was climbed in another three-day trip by Munro and Palmer. They reached the north-east ridge from the Bersaerkerbrae at False Col, overlooking the Skjoldungebrae just west of Kensington, and then traversed three minor summits (all first ascents) before reaching the Hjornespids. The descent was made to the head of the Gully Gletscher by the west ridge.

Other climbs included the Dansketinde (third ascent), Lambeth (second ascent), Glamis (fourth ascent) and Beaumaris (second ascent).

The glaciological work of the expedition included velocity, surface ablation, and strain and surface deformation measurements, all made on the Bersaerkerbrae, also the study of dirt cones on the surface of the glacier.

The expedition suffered two accidents on the Bersaerkerbrae, fortunately without serious consequences. Keith Miller fell into a crevasse on the way up to Col Major and suffered head injuries, including fractures. He was able to walk back to base camp but had to be flown to Mesters Vig by helicopter and on to Reykjavik by Catalina flying boat.

Tom Hird, who was doing glaciological research on the lower Bersaerkerbrae with David Drewry, fell into a glacier stream and was swept down for about a kilometre before being stopped by a large boulder in the bed of the stream. In trying to save him, Drewry also fell in but managed to stop himself and climb out. Hird was pulled out bleeding, semi-conscious and in a state of shock, but he managed to stagger back to base camp. Three weeks later he was able to climb again.

The Dundee University Expedition, led by Iain Smart and Roger Allen, crossed the Mellem Pass and walked down the Schuchert Dal to the Lang Gletscher. There they ascended for the first time its large tributary, the Gannochy Glacier; they discovered at its head an easy pass, the Courier Pass, leading over to the Dalmore Glacier, a tributary of the Roslin Gletscher. Thus a completely new climbing area was opened up on the southern edge of the Cantabrae peaks climbed in 1963. The Dundee climbers made first ascents of nine peaks in the vicinity of the Courier Pass. North of the pass, on the ridge overlooking the Lang Gletscher system, *Dome* and four others were climbed. South of the Courier Pass the *Dreverspitz*, and a short distance further south-west *Bonarbjerg* and *Tunatinde*, were all climbed from the upper part of the Gannochy Glacier.

While these climbs were in progress, the Dundee scientists were studying pingos on the east side of the Schuchert Dal, and Smart was continuing his study of arctic terns breeding on the Menanders Islands.

(*Pingos* are mounds of earth, gravel and boulders which have been forced upward by the thawing–freezing cycle of water and ice lying between the permafrost and surface soil and rock. Pingos may be shaped like cones or ridges, and heights of up to 30 metres have been observed in the Schuchert Dal. The core is composed of ice, and when this melts during the very slow collapse of a pingo a water filled crater may develop near the crest.)

At the beginning of August several small groups of climbers from Europe, sharing a charter flight, arrived at Mesters Vig and went their various ways into the mountains. One party – Robin Chalmers, Norman Tennent, Pat Gunson and

Donald Bennet – went overland to the head of Alpe Fjord, making the first crossing of the Edinbrae and the pass at its head; this was followed two days later by the first crossing from the Lang Gletscher to the Grantabrae, traversing two peaks of the *Diadem*. Later the same party made the third ascent of the *Sefstromstinde* by the south ridge, and two other first ascents – *Tirefour* and *Christinabjerg* – on the north side of the Kirkbrae.

Meanwhile Graham Tiso's party of five sailed round to Alpe Fjord and worked up the Gully Gletscher. There they made the third ascent of the Norsketinde by a new route – a 1200m. snow gully up the middle of the south-east face. Stonefall forced the party on to a rock buttress for the last quarter of the route. Later this party climbed a 2050m. peak overlooking Alpe Fjord on the north side of the Gully Gletscher before crossing the fiord to climb in Nathorsts Land.

A third party of four German climbers led by Hermann Huber, climbed in the Vikingebrae and made several first ascents including *Trespids* on the north side of the glacier, *Hogspids* and *Black Twin* on the south side, and *Pt.2250* close to the Friheds Pass.

The biggest purely mountaineering expedition of 1968 was a French party of sixteen men and women led by Claude Rey. They arrived at Mesters Vig just after the middle of July and were held up for two or three days by ice in Kong Oscars Fjord; however, as soon as this cleared the party moved round to the head of Dammen in two large and powerful inflatable dingies. By the beginning of August the French party was established in a camp about 8km. up the Prinsesse Gletscher.

From this camp, and a higher one about 6km. further up the glacier, the French climbers systematically attacked everything within range. On the east side of the glacier four mountains – *Pic A. Georges, Pic Andersen, Pic Ludovica* and *Mont Frendo* – were climbed by the steep rock and ice routes leading from the Prinsesse directly to their summits. At the head of the Prinsesse two passes – the Col de Scoresby and the Col de Fureső – were reached but not descended on their south sides to the Borgbjerg Gletscher. Two prominent peaks overlooking these cols were also climbed.

On the west side of the Prinsesse the French climbers made several very difficult climbs up the steep ridges and buttresses leading to the ice-cap which at this point was called *Mont Blanc de Fureső*. Two very difficult routes were made up to the ice-cap, one over *Pointe Humbert* and the other up the north face of the *Pointe d'Argent*.

North of Mont Blanc de Fureső the French climbers made a long circuit of the undulating snow domes situated round the head of the Glacier des Oubliettes. One of these domes, the *Dôme du Blizzard*, appears to be the highest point of the ice-cap west of the Prinsesse Gletscher.

The last French climb was a three day epic by J. Fourcy and J. Midière. From the Fureső they ascended the narrow and difficult Glacier des Tours, and climbed the north-west face of the *Tour Vercours*. From there they traversed to the *Tour Chartreuse* and continued southwest along a high ridge at the head of the Glacier des Tours to reach eventually the shoulder of Pic A. Georges from which they descended to the Prinsesse Gletscher.

Several other climbs done by this expedition lasted two or three days, and the French climbers seem to have made the maximum use of the continuous daylight to do very long climbs and traverses.

1969

Toni Gobbi returned to the Staunings Aps in June 1969. As in 1967, he was primarily interested in ski-mountaineering and once again went to the Bersaerkerbrae where ascents of Dunottar, Kensington, Merchistontinde and Col Major were made. One group made a very fine ski traverse by way of the Skel Glacier and Pass, Schuchert Gletscher, Trumpington Col, Lang Gletscher, Churchill Col and Sefstroms Glacier to

Alpe Fjord. The return to the Bersaerkerbrae was made by the Gully Gletscher and Col Major. This must have been a really magnificent ski touring expedition.

1970

In 1970 several small expeditions were in the Staunings Alps. In July the author, with Malcolm Slesser, made a new and easier route on the Bersaerkerspire; they also made the first ascent of the small rock peak to its west.

The route on the Bersaerkerspire was repeated by three members of the Ladies Scottish Climbing Club – Helen Steven, Eilidh Nisbet and Mora Macallum – who were the first all-women party to climb a major Staunings Alp peak.

In August, Claude Rey and his party sailed round to Alpe Fjord and visited the Vikingebrae where five climbs were achieved. These included the fourth ascent of the Norsketinde, this time by the SW couloir (a very difficult ice climb graded TD), and the first ascent of the *Mythotinde* which seems to be the highest peak between the Vikingebrae and the Fangshytte Gletscher.

There was also a Dundee University Expedition in Scoresby Land in 1970. To a large extent this was a scientific expedition, with some parties working as far south as Nordvest Fjord. The climbing group made the Mellem Pass crossing to the Schuchert Dal and Roslin Gletscher. From there they continued south-westwards across the Bjørnbo Gletscher to reach Holger Danskes Briller, a valley on the north side of Nordvest Fjord. On their return journey northwards they visited two previously unexplored glaciers (possibly the Uranus and Aries) and climbed a few virgin peaks, but their exact route is still shrouded in mystery. All that is known with any certainty is that the following year the Lancaster University party found a cairn on a peak just northwest of Karabiner, and a note stating that the first ascent had been made in 1970 by the Dundee party. This peak could well have been climbed in the course of a traverse between the Aries and Bjørnbo glaciers.

A Cambridge expedition led by Keith Miller was also in the Roslin Gletscher in 1970 doing scientific work.

1971

In 1971 a sudden restriction was imposed by the Danish Civil Aviation Authority on landings at Mesters Vig, and only Claude Rey with a small party was permitted to enter. Other parties flew in to Scoresbysund which will continue, as long as present restrictions remain in force, to be the only point of access to the Staunings Alps. Claude Rey's party visited the Vikingebrae again and made the first ascent of a peak about 2km. north of the Velvedes Pass.

A fairly large mountaineering and scientific expedition from Lancaster University used a small boat to travel round from Scoresbysund to the southern end of the Schuchert Dal, and beyond into Nordvest Fjord. The climbing party went up the Bjørnbo Gletscher and made the first ascent of *Yllis*, a small peak near the foot of the glacier, and second ascents of *Karabiner* and *Taurubjerg* at the head of the Leo Glacier. They then went on the head of the Orion Glacier and from the Orion-Borgbjerg col climbed two peaks on the south-west side of the col, named *Albert* and *Lancaster*. The latter mountain appeared to be the highest between the Orion and Borgbjerg glaciers.

Finally, Malcolm Slesser discovered in the Roscoe Bjerge a delightful range of small mountains immediately north of Scoresbysund, and enjoyed excellent ski-mountaineering and some pleasant first ascents.

List of Mountains Climbed

This list is by no means a complete record of all the climbs done in the Staunings Alps. Some expeditions have not reported their climbs, and others have left incomplete records or records that are difficult to interpret. Geologists of Nordisk Mineselskab have climbed many peaks near the Schuchert Dal without reporting them in mountaineering literature.

The names of mountains, passes and glaciers used in this list (and elsewhere in this book) are not all officially approved by the Geodetic Institute of Denmark. There are several important examples of discrepancies: for instance Col Major appears on the latest map as Majorpasset, but the name Col Major is now firmly established among mountaineers. As another example, the Roslin and Lang glaciers are also called the Ivar Baardson Gletscher and the Stor Gletscher respectively. In the case of the mountains, most names proposed by British and other expeditions appear to have been accepted by the Geodetic Institute subject to the addition of the word 'tinde', 'spids', 'bjerge', 'fjell' or 'toppen', all of which mean mountain or peak.

Routes and standards of difficulty are indicated if known, and are taken from original articles and reports. References to such articles and reports are given where possible.

Most of the mountains in this list are marked on the two detailed maps of the Staunings Alps which have been specially drawn for this book. (Maps 4 and 5.) These maps have been prepared from existing maps published by the Geodetic Institute of Denmark, and from expedition reports. The exact position of some of the mountains shown is difficult to infer from some reports, and therefore exact accuracy is not possible.

1950

Swiss Peak; 1769m.; 2km. N.W. of Skel Pass (Pt. 1769m. on map 72 Ø2). Probable route from Schuchert Gletscher up side glacier south of peak; G. Styger. (Second ascent by K. Bryan and D. J. Bennet by N. ridge, 1958). Refs (2), (15).
Kathispids; 1900m.; position uncertain but in the Vikingebrae area; P. Braun and F. Schwartzenbach.

1951

Solvhorn; 1850m.; 11km. S.S.W. of the junction at the foot of the Skjoldungebrae. Ascent (partly on skis) by glacier N. of peak; P. Braun, F. Schwartzenbach.
Frihedstinde; 2610m.; near head of Skjoldungebrae. Ascent from Friheds Pass by snow gully on N.W. of peak; Braun, Schwartzenbach. Ref (1).
Elizabethtinde; 2250m.; between Skjoldungebrae and Dunottar Glacier. Ascent by rocky S.W. ridge; Braun, Schwartzenbach. (Second ascent, from the north, by A. R. Heen, K. Barstad, O. Roed; 1951.) Refs. (1), (8), (9).
Vardefjeld; 1950m.; east side of Skjoldungebrae; Heen, Barstad, Roed. Refs. (8), (9).
Tarnfjeld; 2020m.; E. side of Skjoldungebrae, 3km. S.S.E. of Vardefjeld. Ascent from Skjoldungebrae; Heen, Barstad, Roed. (This is probably the same peak as that attempted from the south by John Hunt's party in 1960, and named Caerleon. The second ascent was made by the Imperial College Expedition, 1963). Refs. (2), (8), (9), (18), (19).

1954

Norsketinde; 2860m.; between Vikingebrae and Gully Gletscher. Ascent from Vikingebrae by Invertebrae and gully on W. side of peak; A. R. Heen, O. Roed, E. Jensen, E. Hoff. (Second ascent W. Diehl and Schwartzenbach by original route, 1954. Third ascent by W. Anderson and B. Hill by S.E.

face, 1968. Fourth ascent by Claude Rey party by S.W. couloir (TD) 1970.) Refs. (2), (9), (10), (12), (28).

Hellefjeld; 1950m.; N. side of Vikingebrae overlooking Alpe Fjord. Heen, Roed, Jensen, Hoff.

Skiferbjerg; 1920m.; S. side of Vikingebrae overlooking Alpe Fjord. Heen, Roed, Jensen, Hoff.

Dansketinde; 2930m.; between head of Gully Gletscher and head of Vikingebrae. Ascent from Gully Gletscher by col E of summit; J. Haller, W. Diehl, F. Schwartzenbach. (Second ascent by G. Monzino's party by N.E. face from head of Vikingebrae, 1964. Third ascent by R. Palmer, T. Hird by original route, 1968.) Refs. (2), (10), (12), (26).

1957

Austrian Expedition. H. Gsellman (leader), H. Kogelbauer, S .Huber, G. Fuchs, K. Gilg, H. Kollensperger, G. Billing, E. Hoff. Refs. (2), (13). (The sketch map in Ref. (13) is none too accurate, and the exact position of some of the Austrian peaks is uncertain.)

Eckhorn; 2230m. At the corner between the Spörre Gletscher and the Furesö. Ascent by N.E. ridge.

Bavariaspids; ca. 2350m. Snow peak at the head of Kirkbrae, overlooking Lang Gletscher. Ascent (partly on skis) by Kirkbrae and N.E. face.

Dreikant; ca. 2400m. Rock and ice peaks between Kirkbrae and Grantabrae. Route unknown. There are two or three distinct peaks and it is not known which one was climbed.

Diadem; ca. 2400m. Three snow peaks at the head of the Grantabrae, overlooking Grantalang Col. Western peak climbed in 1963 by Cambridge party and called Down-ingfjeld. Ascent on ski from head of Grantabrae. (Second ascent of east and centre peaks by D. J. Bennet, R. Chalmers, N. Tennent, P. Gunson from Lang Gletscher, 1968.)

Sefstromstinde; 2800m. Highest mountain on N.E. side of Sefstroms Glacier. Ascent probably by S. Ridge (AD).

(Second ascent by H. Blumer, A. Hofmann, R. Kaiser by N.E. ridge, 1964. Third ascent by D. J. Bennet and P. Gunson, by S. ridge, 1968.)

Sefstromsgipfel; ca. 2720m. Highest mountain at the head of the Sefstroms Glacier. No details known.

Kastenberg; ca. 2400m. Several peaks in a group on the N.W. side of the Cantabrae. Probable route of ascent from Cantabrae.

Kapelle; ca. 1980m. Peak at the corner of the Sefstroms Glacier and the Kirkbrae. Probable ascent from Kirkbrae up S.E. face.

Mitterspids; ca. 2300m. Peak at the junction of Kirkbrae and smaller glacier to N.W. Route not known.

Weisse Wand; ca. 2700m. This peak is shown on the Austrian map as being close to, or just W. of Korsspids. Some doubt as to its true position and the route taken.

Sonnblickspids; 2500m. The Austrian map shows this mountain on the S.E. side of the Knacke Gletscher, but all other maps show it on the N.W. side of this glacier. No details known of the route.

1958

Scottish East Greenland Expedition. C. G. M. Slesser (leader), D. J. Bennet, K. Bryan, R. Cameron, L. Lovat, S. Paterson, C. S. Rose, D. Scott, I. H. M. Smart. Refs. (2), (15).

Glamis; 2200m. First big peak S.W. of Glamis Col. Ascent from Kishmul Glacier to Glamis–Kishmul col, then by S.E. ridge (AD); Slesser, Lovat, Scott, Smart, Cameron. (Second ascent by G. Monzino's party from Bersaerkerbrae, 1963. Third ascent by T. Gobbi's party, 1967. Fourth ascent by R. Palmer and T. Banaszek, by N. ridge, 1968.)

Dunvegan; 1900m. The highest rock peak on the divide between the Skeldal and the lower Bersaerkerbrae. Climbed by the glacier on N. side of peak, and the N. ridge (AD); Bryan, Paterson, Rose.

Dunottar; 2500m. Big mountain at head of Dunottar Glacier. Ascent by N. face (F); Bennet, Smart. (Second ascent by T. Gobbi's party, 1967).

Achnacarry; ca. 2130m. Rock peak at head of Dunottar Glacier 2km. N.N.W. of Dunottar. Ascent by S.E. face (D); Cameron, Slesser.

Merchistontinde; 2400m. Massive peak near head of Bersaerkerbrae, 2km. N.W. of Bersaerkertinde. Ascent from Bersaerkerbrae by N.E. ridge, (AD); Bennet, Paterson. (Second ascent by F. Eckman, T. Friese-Greene, M. Key and J. Taylor, 1963. Third ascent by M. Munro, R. Palmer and E. Williams, 1968. Fourth ascent by T. Gobbi's party, 1969.)

Carrick; 1970m. Twin rock spires on the S.W. side of Dunottar Glacier, 2km. E. of Dunottar. Ascent by gully leading to N. side of peak (D); Bryan, Rose.

Beaufort; ca. 2000m. Rock spire 400m. N.E. of Kapelle near foot of Kirkbrae. Ascent by steep glacier on W. of peak, then S.W. ridge (D); Bryan, Lovat. (The Austrians attempted this peak in 1957, but do not appear to have got to the top.)

Ruthven; ca. 2400m. About 800m. N.E. of Sefstromstinde. Ascent by 900m. gully on S. of peak leading to Ruthven–Sefstromstinde col, then S.W. ridge, (AD); Cameron, Rose.

Tantallon; ca. 2480m. Multi-spired peak 2½km. E.N.E. of Sefstromstinde. Ascent by narrow glacier S.W. of peak (Tantallon Glacier) involving difficult icefall, then up headwall and along W. ridge (AD); Slesser, Smart. (Second ascent by Bennet and Rose, same route. Third ascent by P. Meinherz and W. Thut from Knacke Gletscher, 1964.)

Eilan Donan; ca. 1500m. Rock peak overlooking E. side of Dammen. Ascent direct from Dammen; good, long rock climb (AD); Bryan, Lovat.

Lennox; ca. 1800m. Rock peak on S.W. side of Sefstroms Glacier opposite Sefstromstinde. Ascent from Sefstroms Glacier by S.E. ridge (face), (AD); Bryan, Lovat.

Tioram; ca. 1800m. 1km. S.W. of Lennox. Ascent by E. face (AD); Bryan, Lovat.

Inverarnan; 2000m. Twin-pointed rock peak 1½km. K. of Tioram. Ascent from Krabbe Gletscher and S.E. ridge (AD); Bryan, Lovat. (Second ascent by Bennet and Cameron from Sefstroms Glacier and N. ridge. (PD).)

Roslinborg; 2560m. Big mountain on N. side of Duart–Roslin pass. Ascent direct from pass (F); Slesser, Smart. (Second ascent by G. Schnaidt and P. Schubert by same route, 1966.)

1960

British Greenland Expedition. John Hunt (leader), C. G. M. Slesser, A. Blackshaw, J. A. Jackson, D. Jones, G. Lowe, I. MacNaught-Davis, I. Smart, H. R. A. Streather, J. Sugden, T. Weir and others. Refs. (2), (16), (18).

Harlech; 1900m. Prominent mountain on N.W. of lower Bersaerkerbrae. Ascent by S.E. ridge (F); Hunt, Streather, Jones *et al.*

Elsinore; ca. 1970m. 3km. N.N.E. of Harlech. Climbed from Caerleon Glacier; Blackshaw, Streather. (Second ascent by Imperial College party, 1963.)

Stirling; 1640m. The northernmost peak on the Bersaerkerbrae–Skeldal divide. Climbed from the foot of the Bersaerkerbrae (F); Blackshaw, Streather *et al.* (Second ascent by Imperial College party, 1963.)

Tintagel; ca. 1800m. Rock peak overlooking the 'corner' of the Bersaerkerbrae. Climbed by S.S.W. ridge from good campsite at foot of peak (PD); Slesser, Jackson, Lowe, MacNaught-Davis. (At least three subsequent ascents.)

Beaumaris; ca. 1900m. Pointed rock peak 3km. S.W. of Dunvegan. Ascent by N.W. ridge (PD); Hunt, Jackson. (Second ascent by J. Kanerans, M. Munro, E. Williams by same route, 1968.)

Bersaerkerspire; ca. 2000m. Dramatic rock peak 2½km.

W.N.W. of Tintagel. Ascent by slabs and chimneys of S. face. Excellent rock climb, pitches of V; Slesser, Mac-Naught-Davis. (Several subsequent ascents, including new route up easy-angled ridge S.W. of summit by Slesser and D. J. Bennet, 1970.)

Hjørnespids; 2860m. Ascent by the long S.E. ridge, involving the traverse of many gendarmes, descent by S. ridge (TD); Slesser, MacNaught-Davis. (Second ascent by N.E. ridge, descent by N.W. ridge to Gully Gletscher by M. Munro and R. Palmer, 1968.)

Kilmory; ca. 2100m. Peak at junction of Jupiter and Main glaciers. Probable line of ascent by E. ridge; Blackshaw, F. Baber.

Kilvrough; ca. 2300m. On N.E. side of Bjørnbo Gletscher at Concordia. No details of route except that it was easy; Hunt, Blackshaw.

Pevensey; ca. 2000m. S.S.W. of Kilvrough. Traverse of peak from Kilvrough; Hunt, Blackshaw.

Karabiner; ca. 1850m. Peak at head of Leo Glacier. Ascent by E. ridge, (F); Hunt, Blackshaw, Jackson. (Second ascent by H. Pinkerton, W. Band, P. Taylor; 1971.)

1961

Bangor Junior Mountaineering Club Expedition. M. K. Lyon (leader), R. Barber, M. Petrovsky, B. Roberts, D. Fagan, Brian Brewster, Barry Brewster, D. Daniels, D. Jones.
(This expedition does not appear to have been reported in mountaineering literature, and the following information is based on personal correspondence with Dewi Jones.)

Royal Peak; ca. 2500m. About 1½km. E. of Bersaerkerbrae. Ascent from S.E. via Schuchert Gletscher, no details known; Brewster, Brewster, Daniels, Roberts. (Second ascent by T. Friese-Greene, A. Husselbury, G. Pert and H. Watson from Bersaerkerbrae, 1963.)

1. Camp in upper basin of the Lang Gletscher. On the skyline (right) are the peaks of the Diadem, with (extreme right) Downing Fjeld.

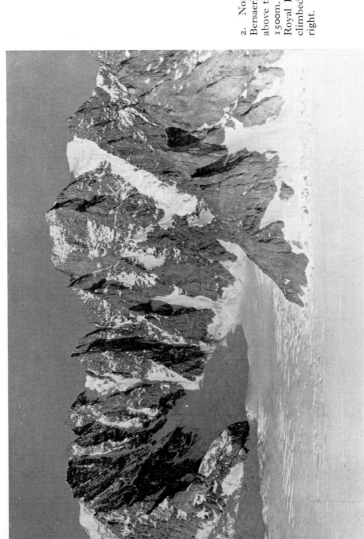

2. North face of the Bersaerkertinde. The face above the glacier is 1200–1500m. high. On the left is Royal Peak, with an unclimbed rock peak to its right.

3. Near head of the Bersaerkerbrae. On left is the Hjornespids, on the right (from left to right) are Kensington, Notting Hill and Bersaerkerspire.

4. Looking towards the head of the Sefstroms Glacier from foot of the Grantabrae.

5. Looking south from Emmanuel. Beyond the unclimbed spire in foreground is the Sefstromsgipfel (on right).

6. Attilaborgen from the Sefstromstinde, looking west towards the Greenland icecap.

7. Sailing along the shore of Kong Oscars Fjord, with the spires of the Syltoppen beyond.

8. Norsketinde from the south. The long gully is the Hill-Anderson route.

9. Junction of the Sefstroms Glacier and the Cantabrae. The three peaks are (left to right) Emmanuel, Sidney and Sussex. In the distance (right) is Cantabrigia.

Point Neurose. This peak is located a short distance S.W. of Royal Peak, but no details of the first ascent are known.

Gauche Peak. This peak is located near Trumpington Col, but no details of the first ascent are known.

Santes Fair; ca.2200m. On S.W. side of Lang Gletscher, near junction of unnamed glacier. Ascent and descent by N. face; Jones, Petrovsky.

Lang Peak 2; ca. 1950m. One of six peaks on N.E. side of Lang Gletscher, Peak 1 being the one at the S.E. end of the line. Ascent from Lang Gletscher; Jones, Petrovsky.

Lang Peak 3; ca. 1950m. Ascent from Lang Gletscher.

Lang Peak 5; ca. 2100m. Ascent from Lang Gletscher; Barber, Fagan, Lyon.

Lang Peak 6; ca. 2100m. Ascent from Lang Gletscher; Jones, Barber, Lyon, Petrovsky.

In addition to the climbs listed above some peaks between the Schuchert and Lang Glaciers were climbed, including the peaks immediately N. and S. of the col W. of Malmberg.

Junior Mountaineering Club of Scotland Expedition. J. Clarkson (leader), H. Brunton, I. Douglas, G. Evans, M. Fleming, G. Hendry, C. Levene, K. Murray, R. Tanton. Refs. (2), (17).

Hermitage; 2040m. Peak between centre and S.E. branches of Mars Glacier. Ascent by S.E. ridge from Mars Glacier (AD); Clarkson, Levene, Douglas, Tanton.

Kilroy; 1520m. Rock peak on S.W. side of Bjørnbo Gletscher, N. of Mercury Glacier. Ascent by N. buttress from foot of Demos Glacier, (D); Murray, Fleming.

Bastille; 1850m. Peak immediately S. of Concordia on Bjørnbo Gletscher. Ascent by N. face (PD); Brunton, Murray, Hendry, Fleming.

Sentinel; 2250m. Prominent mountain at junction of Pegasus and Main glaciers. Ascent by S.E. ridge (F); Clarkson, Douglas, Evans, Tanton.

Pisa; 1350m. Small rock peak overlooking junction of Bjørnbo and Mercury glaciers, on N. side of Mercury. Ascent by N.E. spur (D); easy descent S. to Mercury Glacier; Clarkson, Murray.

Midnight Peak; 1700m. Peak overlooking Mercury Glacier. Ascent by N.E. ridge (PD); Clarkson, Douglas, Evans, Levene.

Citadel; 2000m. On N. side of Mercury Glacier, 2½km. W. of Kilroy. Ascent by S. face to W. peak, traverse to E. peak, descent by S. face, (PD); Clarkson, Douglas, Levene, Murray.

Maclear; 1900m. On N. side of Mercury Glacier, opposite Midnight Peak. Ascent by S. face (PD); Evans, Levene, Murray.

Hermes; 2100m. At head of Mercury Glacier. Ascent from left hand upper cirque of glacier (PD); Clarkson, Douglas, Murray.

First Point of Aries; 1900m. Peak between Mercury and Aries glaciers. Ascent by W. ridge (PD); Clarkson, Douglas, Evans, Murray.

Darien; ca. 2400m. Snow peak on the Spörre–Main glacier divide. Ascent by snow ridge from Darien Pass (F); Brunton, Fleming, Hendry, Tanton.

Edinburgh; 2000m. Peak 1½km. W. of Kilmory. Ascent by S.E. ridge (PD); Clarkson, Douglas, Fleming, Murray.

Zeus; 1850m. Rock peak on S. side of Jupiter Glacier. Ascent by N. face and W. ridge (PD); Brunton, Hendry, Levene, Tanton.

Culross and Dollar; both 2050m. Twin peaks between head of Jupiter and Mercury glaciers. Fine traverse of two peaks (AD); Brunton, Clarkson.

Daedalus; 2040m. Peak at the centre of the group between Mercury and Jupiter glaciers. Ascent by S.W. ridge (F); Hendry, Tanton.

Dinosaur (N. summit); 1900m. Impressive row of rock peaks

at head of Jupiter Glacier. Ascent by N. ridge (AD); Fleming, Murray.

Nevis; 2150m. Peak on Jupiter–Triton glacier divide. Ascent by N. spur (PD); Brunton, Clarkson.

Prometheus; 2570m. The highest mountain of the Jupiter Glacier system, on S.W. side of Orion glacier. Ascent by S. face (PD); Fleming, Hendry, Levene, Tanton.

Blair; 2200m. On S.W. side of Orion Glacier, near junction with Jupiter. Ascent by E. face (PD); Douglas, Murray.

Tent Peak; 2230m. Fine snow-capped rock peak at head of S. branch of Jupiter Glacier. Ascent by E. ridge (PD); Brunton, Clarkson.

Wedge Peak; 2250m. Another fine rock peak, 1km. W. of Tent Peak. Ascent by N. face direct, a magnificent rock climb (TD); descent by rocks on E. side of Tent–Wedge couloir; Fleming, Murray.

Kirriemuir; 2100m. Peak at head of Jupiter Glacier, 2½km. N.W. of Nevis. Ascent by S.E. ridge (PD); Douglas, Hendry, Levene, Tanton.

Tantalus; 2480m. The second highest mountain in the area, at the head of Pegasus Glacier. Ascent by S. face (PD); Clarkson, Brunton, Hendry.

1963

Cambridge East Greenland Expedition. C. F. Knox (leader), A. J. Robinson, J. C. Lendon, C. W. Barlow, C. R. Donaldson Wood, N. J. Estcourt, J. M. Graham, R. E. Hildrew, J. R. Morton, N. H. Pott, R. K. Roschnik, P. F. Rowat. Refs (20), (21).

Knoxtinde (*Grandes Jorasses*); 2750m. Magnificent mountain at head of Bersaerkerbrae, Gully and Schuchert glaciers. Ascent from head of Gully by snow couloir (AD); Knox, Rowat, Pott. (Second ascent by N.E. face from Bersaerkerbrae a few weeks later by F. Eckman, T. Friese-Greene, M. Key, J. Taylor.)

Queenstinde; 2170m. Snow peak on S.W. side of Krabbe Gletscher. Ascent by spur (upper part ice) from Krabbe (AD); Morton, Robinson, Estcourt, Hildrew.

Kings Peak; 2470m. The last big peak on the Sefstroms–Gully divide overlooking Alpe Fjord. Climbed by lowest side glacier on N.E. of Sefstroms (PD); Rowat, Pott, Lendon, Knox.

Sidney; 2300m. The peak overlooking the junction of the Cantabrae and Sefstroms Glacier. Ascent from junction of glaciers by N. face (snow) and N.E. ridge (rock) (AD); Roschnik, Hildrey, Estcourt, Knox, Morton, Pott.

Sussex; 2300m. Sharp rock peak 1km. S.W. of Sidney. Ascent by N.E. ridge from Sidney (AD); Estcourt, Pott.

Emmanuel; 2400m. Impressive rock peak 1200m. S.E. of Sidney. Ascent by N.W. ridge from Sidney (AD); Hildrew, Roschnik, Morton, Knox.

Newnham Tump; 2500m. First peak on Roslin–Cantabrae divide S.W. of Newnham Col. Ascent from Cantabrae via col (AD); Pott, Morton.

Magog; 2600m. Peak at the head of the easternmost of four branches of the Cantabrae. Ascent (partly on skis) from Cantabrae (PD–AD); Estcourt, Hildrew, Roschnik, Rowat.

Snetoppen; 2880m. Massive snow mountain at head of the Cantabrae, the highest S. of Dansketinde. Climbed from Cantabrae by Newnham Col and ice plateau called Parker's Piece (partly on skis) (PD); Robinson, Pott, Knox, Morton.

Pembroke; 2810m. Snow dome at W. side of Parker's Piece. Climbed via Newnham Col and Snetoppen (AD); Robinson, Pott, Knox, Morton.

Downingfjeld; 2500m. Big snow mountain at head (south) of Grantabrae. Ascent (partly on skis) by N. ridge (F); Pott, Morton, Robinson. (This mountain may have been climbed by the Austrians in 1957.)

Trinity; 2840m. Magnificent rock peak on Cantabrae – Krabbe divide. Ascent from Cantabrae by snow gully to Trinity–Snetoppen col, and S.W. ridge (D); Estcourt, Hildrew, Roschnik, Rowat.

Attilaborgen; 2670m. The northernmost of the big peaks on the S.W. side of the Sefstroms Glacier. Ascent by Tioram Glacier and N. face (D); Morton, Knox, Robinson, Pott.

Proctor's Pinnacle; 2350m. Fine looking pinnacle at corner of Vertebrae and Gully Gletscher. Ascent from Gully (AD); Roschnik, Estcourt.

Magdalene; 2500m. The highest peak W. of the Vertebrae on N. side of Gully Gletscher. Ascent by S. face from foot of Vertebrae (D); Roschnik, Estcourt.

Selwyn; 2140m. The highest peak W. of Magdalene. Climbed from Gully by small glacier W. of Vertebrae to reach S. ridge (PD); Estcourt, Robinson.

Bolvaerket; 2500m. Fine isolated peak at head of Gully Gletscher. Ascent by ice gully on E. face, followed by S.E. ridge, (D–TD); Morton, Roschnik.

Gonville and *Caius*; both ca. 2280m. Two sharp rock summits on W. side of Cavendish Glacier. Both summits climbed by E. faces with traverse between them (PD); Graham, Donaldson Wood.

Clare; ca. 2220m. Snow peak about 800m. W.N.W. of Caius. Ascent by rock rib on E. face (PD); Graham, Donaldson Wood.

St John's Peak; ca. 2200m. Rock peak on N.E. side of Cavendish Glacier. Ascent by S.E. ridge (PD); Knox, Graham.

Homerton; 2360m. Snow bump at head (west) of Cavendish Glacier. Ascent from Cavendish Glacier (F); Donaldson Wood, Graham, Hildrew, Knox.

Korsspids; ca. 2780m. Massive mountain at head (east) of Cavendish Glacier. Climbed by col at head of glacier and S.W. ridge (AD); Donaldson Wood, Graham, Hildrew, Knox. (It is not clear if this peak was climbed by the Austrians in 1957. There was no sign of a previous ascent, and the Austrians may have climbed the next mountain to the S.E. which is slightly lower.)

Cantabrigia; 2780m. Fine looking mountain at the head of the Cantabrae. Ascent by prominent ice shelf across N. face, followed by ice gully above (AD); Barlow, Lendon, Pott, Rowat.

Girton; 2360m. First peak on Kirkbrae–Lang Gletscher divide S.E. of Churchil Col. Ascent from col by snow ridge (F); Barlow, Lendon, Pott, Rowat.

St Bartholomew's Tower; 2440m. Rock peak with twin summits S.W. of Crescent Col. Ascent of S. summit by gully in E. face from head of Lang Gletscher (AD); Barlow, Lendon, Pott, Rowat.

Imperial College East Greenland Expedition. M. H. Key (leader), F. Ekman, T. W. Friese-Greene, A. Husselbury, J. Lovering, G. J. Pert, J. Taylor, H. D. D. Watson. Ref (19).

Elephant; ca. 1830m. Rock peak at head of Caerleon Glacier. Ascent by S. face; Lovering, Taylor.

Castle; ca. 1830m. Another rock peak at the head of Caerleon Glacier. Ascent by S. face, pitches of IV; Friese-Greene, Husselbury, Lovering, Taylor.

Piccadilly; 1720m. On divide between Bersaerkerbrae and Skeldal, 1½ km. N. of Dunvegan. Ascent by E. ridge, bad rock; Key, Watson.

Bow; 1700m. Rock peak on Harlech Glacier–Skjoldungebrae divide. Ascent by S.E. ridge; Ekman, Key.

Vauxhall; ca. 2140m. Rock peak 1½km. S.E. of Elizabethtinde. Ascent by N.E. ridge from Harlech Glacier. Ekman, Key.

Pimlico; ca. 1850m. Rock peak overlooking junction of Dunottar Glacier and Bersaerkerbrae. Ascent by N.E. ridge; Key, Ekman.

Poplar; ca. 1850m. Rock peak 1½km. N.E. of Pimlico. Ascent by E. face; Ekman, Key.

Blackwall; ca. 1850m. Rock peak about 800m. S.E. of Poplar. Ascent by S.S.E. ridge; Ekman, Key.

Lambeth; ca. 2450m. Big peak on Gully Gletscher–Bersaerkerbrae divide 2km. S. of Col Major. Ascent from Col

Major by N. ridge over smaller summit; Ekman, Friese-Greene, Key, Taylor. (Second ascent by same route; M. Munro, E. Williams; 1968.)

Notting Hill; ca. 2400m. Rock peak 1½km. W.N.W. of Bersaerkerspire. Ascent from upper Bersaerkerbrae; Friese-Greene, Husselbury.

Kensington; ca. 2600m. The highest mountain on the ridge running N.E. then E. from Hjornespids. Ascent from upper Bersaerkerbrae; Watson, Pert. (Owing to some confusion in Ref. (19) the names of these two mountains may be the wrong way round, however their identity is not in doubt. They are the two major peaks between False Col and the Bersaerkerspire.) (Second ascent by T. Gobbi's party, 1969.)

Kishmul; ca. 2450m. Big mountain between Glamis and Royal Peak. Ascent from Bersaerkerbrae by steep, crevassed glacier to reach subsidiary N. summit, then to main top. Friese-Greene, Husselbury, Pert, Watson.

Wapping; 1680m. Peak about 800m. S.W. of Stirling. Ascent from lower Bersaerkerbrae over Stirling; Lovering, Taylor.

Richmond; 1650m. Rock peak between Kishmul Glacier and Edinbrae. Ascent route not known; Ekman, Key.

(There is some doubt as to whether *Caerleon* (named by Hunt) and Tarnfjeld are the same mountain or not. If not, the first ascent of Caerleon was made by Friese-Greene, Husselbury, Key, Watson by the E. ridge.)

1964

Guido Monzino's Expedition. Refs (6), (7).

Cima Ouest; 2400m. Westernmost of two fine rock peaks on S. side of Vikingebrae, W. of Invertebrae. Ascent by side glacier N.W. of peak followed by N.W. ridge.

Cima Est; 2400m. About 800m. east of Cima Ouest. Ascent by side glacier N.N.W. of peak followed by N. ridge.

Academischer Alpen-Club Zurich Expedition. A. Hoffmann (leader), N. Baumann, M. Schmid, W. Thut, H. Weber, H.

Riedhauser, H. Blumer, R. Kaiser, K. Herwig, P. Meinherz. Refs (22), (23), (24). (No heights are quoted in the Swiss report, and heights given below are taken where possible from maps.)

Weydmannsburg; ca. 2700m. The Swiss report shows this peak a short distance S.E. of Korsspids. The route of ascent appears to have been up the Knacke Gletscher and S.W. side of peak. Herwig, Baumann, Weber.

Barenzahne. On N.W. side of Knacke Gletscher. Approach from this glacier and up S.W. side of peak. Meinherz, Thut.

Cerberus. On N. side of Knacke Gletscher, about 800m. W. of Barenzahne. Same approach. Meinherz, Thut.

Unnamed pinnacle W of Weydmannsburg. This pinnacle appears to be situated at the head of the Cavendish Glacier. Ascent from head of Knacke Gletscher by E. ridge. Herwig, Baumann, Weber.

Helmspitzen; ca. 2400m. Rock peak about 2 km. S.W. of Kastenberg. Ascent by S.E. face from Cantabrae. Hoffmann, Blumer, Kaiser.

Pyramid Peak; ca. 2150m. Very fine and prominent rock peak at S.W. corner of Dammen. Ascent by N.W. ridge; Baumann, Thut.

Piz Vadian; 1640m. Peak on N.E. side of Spörre Gletscher overlooking Dammen. Ascent from S.E.; Meinherz, Weber, Herwig.

Piz Spescha; 2210m. Peak on N.E. side of Spörre Gletscher opposite junction of Hecate Glacier. Ascent by S.W. spur direct from glacier; Blumer, Kaiser.

Mont Saussure; 2500m. Big mountain on N.E. side of Duart Glacier. Ascent by S. ridge; Blumer, Meinherz, Herwig, Kaiser. (Second ascent in 1966 by I. Rost, K. Lindner.)

Piz Coaz; 2000m. Narrow ridge between Spörre and Duart glaciers, this seems to be the N.W. peak of the ridge. Ascent along N.W. ridge; Meinherz, Weber, Herwig. (Second ascent in 1966 by members of Herrligkoffer's party.)

Silberspitzen; 2520m. Two or three peaks on ridge between Spörre and Hecate glaciers. Ascent from Spörre Gletscher, approaching peaks from S.E.; Baumann, Weber, Herwig. (Second ascent in 1966 by K. Lindner, P. Schubert.)

Piz Dominant; 2370m. Rock peak 2km. N.N.W. of Silberspitzen in junction of Spörre and Hecate glaciers. Ascent from Spörre Gletscher to reach S ridge; Baumann, Weber, Hoffmann. (Second ascent in 1966 by K. Lindner, P. Schubert.)

Piz Guarda Monti and *Strittberg*; both ca. 1840m. These two peaks, 1km apart, are on the S.W. side of Spörre Gletscher, between it and Pollux Glacier. Ascent of both by N.W. side from Spörre; Meinherz, Hoffmann.

1966

German Expedition to the Staunings Alps. K. Herrligkoffer (leader), M. Anderl, E. Huttl, I. Rost, G. Schnaidt, G. Schweiger, G. Plangger, J. Anzenberger, K. Lindner, P. Schubert. Refs. (3), (25) (The following information is based on Ref. (3). The map in this report is not very accurate and some doubt exists in the author's mind as to the exact position of some of the peaks. Heights given in the report are considerably higher than those on map 71 Ø 2, and heights quoted below are taken where possible from this map.)

Kieferner Toppen; 2430m. Peak on the S. side of the Roslin-Duart Col. Ascent by gully in N.W. face followed by N. ridge; Anzenberger, Plangger.

Tolzersspids; 2430m. *Pleinting Bjerg*; 2290m. Peaks on S. side of Roslin Gletscher near its head. Ascent by N.W. side of col between peaks from which both were climbed; Anderl, Anzenberger, Plangger.

Munchner Tinde; 2550m. Big mountain at head of Spörre and Duart glaciers. Ascent (two parties) by N.W. ridge and by N.E. face; Anderl, Anzenberger, Herrligkoffer, Plangger.

Ulmer Spids and *Augsburger Spids*; both 2500m. Two peaks on ridge N. of Roslinborg. Traverse of ridge from Roslinborg over the two summits; Schnaidt, Schubert.

Priener Kalotte and *Priener Spids*; both 2180m. Two small peaks immediately W. of Roslin – Duart Col. Ascent from col by E. side; Anderl, Herrligkoffer.

Berchtesgadener Tinde; 2530m. *Mittenwalder Tinde*; 2500m. *Lenggrieser Ryggen*; 2530m. These three snow peaks form the southern rim of the Spörre Gletscher's upper basin. Traverse from W. to E. along snow ridge; Anderl, Anzenberger, Plangger.

Muhldorfer Spids; 2430m. Small snow peak S. of Darien Pass on Spörre – Main Glacier divide. Ascent from Spörre Gletscher; Lindner.

Berggeist spids; 2620m. Highest peak on S.W. rim of Spörre Gletscher basin. Ascent from E.; Lindner, Schubert.

Castor; 2440m. Steep peak 1½km. S.E. of Berggeistspids. Ascent from S.E., rock pitches of V; Lindner, Schubert.

Zwerg Spids; 2350m. Small snow peak in S.E. corner of upper basin of Spörre Gletscher. Ascent from N.W.; Schubert.

Kemptner Horn; 2250m. Peak between Roslin and Mars glaciers. Ascent from N.W. side; Lindner, Schubert.

Fussener Ryggen; ca. 2140m. *Lindauer Hornli*; ca. 2070m. *Granit Spids*; ca. 2160m. *Steinbjerg*; ca. 2070m. *Garmischer Spids*; ca. 2200m. These peaks appear to be on the divide between the Roslin Gletscher and the head of the Mars Glacier. Traversed from N. to S.; Lindner, Schubert.

Stuttgarter Spids; 2330m. Snow peak 1½km. E.S.E. of Donnau Passet. Ascent by N. ridge; Anderl, Plangger, Schnaidt.

Leutkirchner Tinde; 2470m. *Kocheler Spids*; 2350m. *Rommelshausener Spids*; ca. 2470m. These three peaks are on a ridge running N.–S. between the Roslin and Main glaciers 5 km. E. of Darien Pass. Traverse of peaks from S. to N.; Anderl, Plangger, Schnaidt.

Sendlinger Kalotte; 2300m. *Sendlinger Bjerg*; 2330m. These two peaks, joined by a narrow ridge, are the highest points of the group between the Spörre and Duart glaciers. Ascent by E. face of Kalotte, traverse S.E. to Bjerg, descent by S. ridge; Schnaidt, Rost.

1967

German (Berchtesgaden) Expedition to the Staunings Alps. Sepp Kurz, Hermann Ponn, Hans Richter, Carl de Temple. The author has seen no written account of this expedition, and the following list of peaks climbed is taken from the map produced by the climbers. No details of routes are known. From aerial photographs the Hecate Glacier looks easy near its head, but the Castor and Pollux glaciers are badly crevassed and look rather difficult.

Sidneytinde; 2500m. This peak is at the head of the Castor Glacier. From aerial photographs it seems to be a massive flat-topped mountain.

Glatze; 2550m. About 1½km. E.S.E. of Sidneytinde, this peak is at the head of the ridge separating the Castor and Pollux glaciers.

Toni Kurz Spids; 2500m. *Hirschbichler Spids*; 2420m. *Wellenkamp Spids*; 2450m. These three peaks are on the N.–S. ridge separating the Castor and Pollux glaciers, the last named being the northernmost.

Hermann von Barth Tinde; 2680m. *Zuckerhutl*; 2410m. *Thurweiser Kopf*; 2360m. These three peaks are on a ridge running S.S.E. from Glatze, overlooking the head of the Pollux Glacier, to the Hecate Glacier.

Berchtesgadener Kopf; 2350m. This top is on the snowy divide between the head of the Hecate Glacier and the Glacier du Renard (a tributary of the Prinsesse Glacier.) Its ascent from the Hecate Glacier (by which the ascent was doubtless made) appears from aerial photographs to be easy.

Schneekuppe; 2640m. This massive mountain with a flat snow-cap lies between the Spörre and Prinsesse glaciers.

Purtscheller Tinde; 2630m. A big snow-capped mountain at the triple divide between the Hecate, Spörre and Prinsesse glaciers. The ascent from the head of the Hecate Glacier appears from aerial photographs to be easy.

Kederbacher Spids; 2560m. and 2440m. Two rock peaks on the Spörre-Hecate divide about 1200m. N.N.E. of the Purtscheller Tinde.

Panoramic Peak; ca. 1680m. This small peak about 800m. N. of Glamis Col was climbed by Toni Gobbi's party.

1968

German (Munich) Expedition to the Staunings Alps. Hermann Huber, Rudi Berger, Horst Schurer, Gunther Fluhrer. The following information is taken from Ref (29).

Trespids; 2000m. to 2100m. Three rock peaks on a N.–S. ridge on the N. side of the Vikingebrae. Traverse of three peaks from S. to N. descent by W. side; Berger, Schurer, Fluhrer.

Pt. 2250m. This unnamed peak is on the N.W. side of the Friheds Pass at the head of the Friheds Glacier. Ascent by S.W. ice-face; Berger, Schurer, Fluhrer.

Hogspids; 2100m. *Black Twin*; 2100m. These two peaks are at the head of the Munich Glacier on the S. side of the Vikingebrae. (This glacier was also climbed for the first time.) Ascent of both peaks from the col between them at the head of the glacier; Berger, Schurer, Fluhrer.

Pt. 1750m. This unnamed peak is on the N. side of the Vikingebrae, W. of Trespids. Ascent from Vikingebrae; Huber.

Scottish Expedition to the Staunings Alps. C. Allan, D. Bennet, R. Chalmers, P. Gunson, D. Jones, M. Slesser, N. Tennent. Ref. (28).

Christinabjerg; ca. 2350m. Peak on N. side of Kirkbrae about

800m. W. of Churchill Col. Ascent by S.E. face from **Kirk-brae**; Bennet, Gunson.

Tirefour; ca. 2140m. Rock tower between Beaufort and Tantallon on N.W. side of Kirkbrae. Ascent by S.E. face, difficult rock pitches on final tower; Gunson, Slesser.

Queen Mary College (London) Expedition. K. Miller (leader), R. Palmer, T. Hird, M. Munro, D. Drewry, T. Banaszek, E. Williams, J. Kanerans. Ref. (26).

Bersaerkertinde; ca. 2620m. The dominent peak at the head of the Bersaerkerbrae. Ascent over the summit of Merchiston and along the connecting (N.W.) ridge, very long climb (D), descent by same route; Munro, Palmer, Williams.

Bosigran, Lamorna, Treyarnon; all ca. 2680m. Three pinnacles on the N.E. ridge of the Hjornespids. Traverse from False Col to Hjornespids; Munro, Palmer.

Dundee University Scoresby Land Expedition. I. H. M. Smart, R. Allen (leaders), A. Pettit, R. O'Brien, R. Heywood, Carvell. Ref. (27). Heights are taken from map 71 Ø 2.

Bonarbjerg; ca. 2200m. Highest mountain on S. side of Gannochy Glacier. Ascent from Gannochy by E. ridge. Pettit, Carvell, Heywood, O'Brien.

Tunatinde; ca. 2000m. Peak about 1km. N.E. of Bonarbjerg. Ascent from Gannochy by W. ridge.

Dreverspids; ca. 2200m. Peak at the head of Gannochy Glacier on S. side of Courier Pass. Ascent from snowbowl N.E. of peak to E. ridge; Pettit, Heywood, Carvell, O'Brien.

The Dome; ca. 2340m. Snow mountain 2½km. N. of Courier Pass. Ascent from Courier Pass by S. ridge, easy; Pettit, Heywood, Carvell, O'Brien.

Dudhope; ca. 2200m. Peak 1½km. S.E. of the Dome. Ascent from Courier Pass by W. ridge; Heywood, O'Brien, Carvell.

Claverhouse; ca. 2300m. Rock summit a short distance E.S.E.

of Dudhope. Ascent by W. ridge from Dudhope; Heywood, O'Brien, Carvell.

The Molehill; ca. 1980m. Small peak 2½km. N.N.W. of Courier Pass. Ascent from Dalmore Glacier by easy rock buttress.

The Wedge; ca. 2160m. Peak about 800m. N.W. of the Dome. Ascent from Dalmore Glacier by ice gully to col N.W. of summit. Pettit, Heywood, O'Brien.

The Pinnacle; ca. 2220m. Peak immediately N. of the Mole-hill. Ascent as for Molehill, then up S. ridge; good rock (IV).

French Expedition to North-East Greenland, 1968. C. Rey (leader), J. Fourcy, J. Midière, F. Valla, J. L. Georges, M. Arnold, B. Thibaudon, H. Brondel, P. Léopold, B. Genand, C. Holé, Mlle M. Boymond, Mlle M. Bogeat, Mme P. Bogeat, Mme S. Georges, Mlle D. Parrot. Ref. (30).

Pic André Georges; 2500m. The first big mountain on E. side of Prinsesse Gletscher. Ascent by W.N.W. buttress direct from glacier (D); M. Bogeat, Boymond, Brondel, Fourcy, Thibaudon, J. L. Georges.

Pic Andersen; 2450m. Peak at the head of Castor Glacier overlooking Prinsesse. Ascent by W. flank and N. ridge (D); Arnold. Holé, Midière, Valla.

Pic Ludovica; 2400m. Twin peak of Pic Andersen, a short distance S. of it. Ascent by W. ridge (AD); M. Bogeat, Parrot, Brondel, Fourcy, Léopold, Midière.

Mont Frendo; 2480m. Isolated mountain on E. side of Prin-sesse. Ascent by W. ridge (D); descent E. from summit and then S. to Glacier du Renard. S. Georges, J. L. Georges, Boy-mond, Arnold, Genand, Rey, Thibaudon, Valla.

Le Casque; 2450m. Rounded snow peak at head of Prinsesse Gletscher. Traverse from W. to E. (AD); P. Bogeat, S. Georges, J. L. Georges, Boymond, Brondel, Léopold.

Tour des Camaieux; 2540m. Rock peak at head of Prinsesse Gletscher, 1½km. E.N.E. of Le Casque. Ascent by W. ridge (AD); S. Georges, J. L. Georges, Boymond, Brondel.

Pic Flotard; 2290m. The summit of the rock promontory between the Prinsesse Gletscher and the Glacier des Violettes. Ascent by N.E. face, (TD); Arnold, Valla.

Dôme de l'Envoi; 2400m. Culminating point of the ice-cap just S. of Pic Flotard. Ascent by ridge from Pic Flotard; Arnold, Valla.

Mont Blanc de Furesö; 2540m. The highest point of the ice-cap overlooking the Prinsesse Gletscher above the confluence of the Glacier des Violettes. Ascent by E. ridge over *Pointe Humbert* (D); M. Bogeat, Holé, Rey, Thibaudon.

Mont Blanc de Furesö was also climbed by the N. pillar of the *Pointe d'Argent,* 2490m, which is the terminal point of the ice-cap 1½km. N. of Mont Blanc de Furesö (TD); descent by the N.E. ridge of Pointe d'Argent (AD); Arnold, Fourcy, J. L. Georges, Midière.

Tour du Pavot; 1750m. Rock tower overlooking W. side of Prinsesse just N. of Combe d'Argent. Ascent by E. face, entirely on rock (D); S. Georges, J. L. Georges, Fourcy, Thibaudon.

Cirque d'Acropole; This cirque of snow domes encloses the Glacier des Oubliettes (just north of the Combe d'Argent) and in its centre rises the rock-fronted promontory called L'Acropole. The traverse was done from *L'Acropole,* 2200m., north to the *Dôme du Trappeur,* 2600m., then W. to the *Dôme du Blizzard,* 2700m., then S. to *Dôme des Séracs,* 2650m., S.E. to *Dôme du Léopard,* 2500m. and finally down N. to *L'Acropole;* Parrot, Brondel, Genand, Léopold, Valla.

Tour Vercours, Tour Chartreuse; both 2500m. Two very steep rock peaks at the head of the Glacier des Tours. Ascent by Glacier des Tours, N.W. face of Tour Vercours, traverse to Tour Chartreuse and along ridge at head of Glacier des Tours to reach shoulder of Pic André Georges, from where the descent was made (TD); complete traverse took three days; Fourcy, Midière.

1970

Dundee University Scoresby Land Expedition. It is reported that eight peaks, six of them first ascents, were made in the area south-west of the Bjørnbo Gletscher. The following is the only one of which details are known to the author:

Taurubjerg; 1860m. 1km. N.W. of Karabiner at head of Leo Glacier. Route unknown; Dundee University party led by R. Haywood. (Second ascent by H. Pinkerton, W. Band, P. Taylor; 1971.)

Other small expeditions made the following first ascents:

West Peak of Bersaerkerspire; 1950m. Ascent by ledges on S. face to breche W. of summit; M. Slesser, D. J. Bennet.

Unnamed peak on Dunottar Glacier between Elizabethtinde and Vauxhall; 2200m. Ascent by S.E. buttress and E. ridge, good rock (D); Mlle. J. Sion, L. Desrivières, C. Rey.

Unnamed peak between Beaumaris and Piccadilly; 1750m. Ascent by W. ridge, mixed snow and poor rock (D); Mlle J. Sion, M. Joubert.

Slanstinde; 2350m. Rock peak on S. side of Vikingebrae. (Exact position uncertain and may be well to the E. of Invertebrae and not to the E. of Munich Gletscher as reported by Claude Rey.) Ascent by E. face (D); C. Dalphin, M. Ebneter, R. Habersaat.

Tour Carrée; 2250m. Peak on watershed between the Friheds and Sedgwick glaciers. Ascent by S.E. buttress, good rock (AD); C. Dalphin, M. Ebneter, J. M. Leroux, A. Sestier.

Mythotinde; 2300m. Peak on the watershed between Vikingebrae and Fangshytte Gletscher, the highest in the area. Ascent by S. face (PD); M. Ebneter, C. Rey.

The ascent of another peak named *Pointe Michel Gravost* was also reported, but Claude Rey considers that it was probably one of the Trespids climbed in 1968 by H. Huber's party.

1971

Lancaster University Expedition. This expedition, which operated in the South Staunings and along the shores of Nordvest Fjord, was principally scientific, but a few of its members did some climbing.

Yllis; 1860m. Peak overlooking Schuchert Dal between Roslin and Bjørnbo glaciers. Ascent by W. Band.

Albert; 2300m, *Lancaster*; 2510m. These two peaks are S.W. of the Orion – Borgbjerg Col. Ascent by ridge from col; H. Pinkerton, W. Band, P. Taylor.

Unnamed peak at the head of the Vikingebrae, 1½ km. N. of Helvedes Pass. Ascent by Claude Rey and party, no further details known.

List of Passes

As already mentioned, most of the glaciers are connected to each other by cols or passes and these make possible a great variety of trans-mountain routes. Some of these routes are important in that they provide access from Mesters Vig to Alpe Fjord and other parts of the Staunings Alps. All are of great interest and beauty.

In this section these passes are summarised, with a note as to their difficulty. At the end of the section mention is made of other passes which have not yet been crossed or which may have been reached from one side only. These passes will doubtless at some time in the future become part of the network of routes that are being discovered in the Staunings Alps.

Gefion Pass (ca. 500m.). This is the easy tundra and gravel covered pass between Mesters Vig and the Skeldal.

Mellem Pass (ca. 800m.). This pass in the Werner Bjerge is between the Mellem and Arcturus glaciers. Easy snow on both sides, although the Mellem side has occasionally been reported to be icy and crevassed.

Skel Pass (ca. 800m.). This pass between the Skel and Schuchert is easy snow on both sides.

Glamis Col (ca. 1100m.). This pass lies between the Kishmul Glacier and the Bersaerkerbrae and is easy snow on both sides. In certain circumstances it might give the shortest route from Mesters Vig to the upper Bersaerkerbrae.

Unnamed pass at the head of the Edinbrae (ca. 1200m.) leading to the Schuchert Gletscher. Easy snow on both sides. There may be another similar crossing 2km. west of this pass.

Friheds Pass (ca. 1800m.). This pass between the Skjoldungebrae and the Friheds Glacier is at the foot of the north-west side of the Frihedstinde. It is fairly easy on the Skjoldungebrae side, but there is a steep drop on the Friheds side which may be icy late in summer.

Col Major (Majorpasset) (ca. 2150m.). Between the Bersaerkerbrae and the Gully Gletscher, this pass is the key to the traverse through the centre of the Staunings Alps. It is easy on the Gully side, but on the other side a steep gully, 400–500 m., drops to the Bersaerkerbrae. This gully is likely to be very icy late in summer, and there is a risk of stonefall.

Wordie Pass (ca. 900m.). This fairly easy pass is between the Vertebrae and the Invertebrae and provides a useful connection between the Gully Gletscher and the Vikingebrae.

Trumpington Col (ca. 1800m.). This pass connects the Schuchert and Lang glaciers. The final snow slopes on both sides are short and steep, and the icefall 1½km. below the col on the Schuchert side is bypassed on the (true) right.

Crescent Col (ca. 2100m.). Between the Lang and Gully glaciers on the south-east side of Bolvaerket, this col is easy snow on both sides.

Churchill Col (ca. 2140m.). This col is between the Lang Gletscher and the Kirkbrae (Sefstroms Glacier). There are snow gullies on both sides, that on the Kirkbrae side being quite steep for about 100m.

Grantalang Col (ca. 2100m.). This col is situated between the Lang Gletscher and the Grantabrae; there are steep snow gullies on both sides, with some stonefall danger.

Ice Col (ca. 1500m.). This col is about 8km. west-north-west of Malmberg and connects the Schuchert Gletscher with a tributary of the Lang. It provides a short cut from the Schuchert to the Lang when approaching from the north.

Courier Pass (ca. 1800m.). This pass at the head of the Gannochy Glacier leads over to the Dalmore Glacier. Easy snow on the Gannochy side, steeper rock wall and snow/ice on the Dalmore side.

Duart-Roslin Col (ca. 2140m.). This pass connecting the

Duart and Roslin glaciers is easy on both sides, although the Duart side is heavily crevassed.

Darien Pass (ca. 2140m.). This easy snow pass connects the Main and Spörre glaciers.

Plinganser Col (ca. 2140m.). This easy snow pass connects the Roslin and Spörre glaciers.

Donnau Passet (ca. 2140m.). This pass connects the upper reaches of the Roslin and Main glaciers.

The following passes and cols have not been traversed, although some of them have been reached from one side. Others have not (to the writer's knowledge) been ascended on either side; however, they are of sufficient importance to merit a mention and will probably be traversed before long.

Helvedes Pass. This is the name given to the lowest point on the divide between the Skjoldungebrae and the Vikingebrae south-south-east of the Frihedstinde. It has been reached from the Vikingebrae but not from the other side.

False Col. This is the col on the Bersaerkerbrae – Skjoldungebrae divide between Hjornespids and Kensington. It has been climbed by a steep snow gully on the Bersaerkerbrae side.

Schuchert–Gully Col. There appears to be a possible col at the head of the Schuchert Gletscher about 1½km. south of the Knoxtinde. On the Schuchert side there are one or two snow gullies that do not seem unduly steep.

Gully–Lang Col. There is a definite col on the west side of Bolvaerket but no record of any crossing. The Lang side of this col appears to be a rather steep snow gully.

Sefstroms–Lang Col. At the head of the Sefstroms Glacier there is an obvious col separating it from an unnamed branch of the Lang Gletscher. There is no record of any crossing although the Austrians in 1957 may have reached the col from the Sefstroms side There appear to be steep snow-ice slopes on both sides.

Newnham Col (ca. 2300m.). This col, at the head of the Cantabrae, was climbed from that side by the Cambridge party in 1963, over easy snow. No descent has been made southwards on the Roslin side; however, this descent was reported to appear easy.

Col de Furesö (ca. 1800m.). This col at the head of the Prinsesse Gletscher is to the north-east of Le Casque. On the Prinsesse side the col is reached by fairly steep snow slopes. No descent has been made southwards to the Borgbjerg Gletscher.

Col de Scoresby (ca. 1800m). This col is on the south-west side of Le Casque, but in all other respects it seems to be very similar to the Col de Furesö, although the south side appears to be rather steep.

Orion–Borgbjerg Col. This col, ca. 2100m., between the head of the Orion Glacier and the upper basin of the Borgbjerg, has been reached easily from the south-east. The north-west side appears from aerial photographs to be easy also.

In the South and West Staunings there must be many unexplored passes. Possible passes have been reported between the Jupiter and Triton glaciers, between the Mercury and Aries glaciers, and between the Mercury and Uranus glaciers. These are just three of the many passes that exist between the Roslin, Bjørnbo and Borgbjerg glacier systems.

Future Climbing Prospects

In 1970 the author, during a visit to Malmberg, was assured by the Austrian geologists working there that all the mountains of the Staunings Alps had been climbed already. This, however, is fortunately not true, and an attempt will be made in this chapter to summarise the possibilities for future first ascents. The author apologises in advance to any party which, inspired by his advice, climbs a mountain expecting a first ascent and finds a cairn on top. He has had this disappointment several times himself.

The *Syltoppen* and *Murchison Bjerge* are not likely to offer much in the way of good first ascents. The former have been well explored, and the latter are not in general very climbworthy.

The Bersaerkerbrae has been pretty well climbed out, but one worthwhile first ascent would be the big pinnacle (almost a separate mountain) between *Bersaerkertinde* and *Royal Peak*. There are also one or two small rock peaks between *Bersaerkerspire* and *Kensington*.

The Vikingebrae has also received a lot of attention, but the outliers of the *Frihedstinde* and *Norsketinde,* none of them a very distinct peak in its own right, will provide some first ascents. The ridge between the *Norkestinde* and *Dansketinde* has one or two minor unclimbed peaks, and there are many rock spires and pinnacles in this area that are probably best attacked from the Gully Gletscher.

On the Gully Gletscher itself there is a formidable row of rock peaks on the ridge running northwards from *Korsspids* (on the east side of the Cavendish Glacier). These will call for rock climbing of a very high standard. There is also room for exploration in the glacier basin between *Korsspids* and *Bolvaerket*; the pass leading over to the Lang Gletscher has yet to be crossed, and there are some unclimbed peaks including the western outlier of *Bolvaerket* and (possibly) some peaks between *Korsspids* and Churchill Col. There is also no record of an ascent of the peak immediately to the east of Crescent Col.

The Sefstroms Glacier, despite all the attention it has received, still has the most attractive prizes in the Staunings Alps for the searcher after unclimbed mountains: these are the two mountains of about 2700m. between *Trinity* and *Attilaborgen*. This whole ridge of four mountains forms a high and jagged wall between the Sefstroms and Krabbe glaciers. The Cambridge climbers in 1963 reported no feasible routes on the Krabbe side, so the most likely route will be from the Sefstroms, starting from the little glacier west of Kastenberg, and will involve 1500m. of continuously steep rock, snow and ice. Elsewhere on the Sefstroms there are several unclimbed peaks round the Cantabrae (two to the west and one to the east of *Cantabrigia*), two or three more between *Emmanuel* and *Sefstromsgipfel,* and the group between *Downingfjeld* and *Sefstromsgipfel.* Someone should also traverse *Dreikant* as it is unlikely that the Austrians climbed all the tops. There seems little doubt that a strong party could collect up to ten very fine virgin peaks in this magnificent area.

In the east there is little left unclimbed. One peak that comes to mind is the highest of the group at the head of the Edinbrae, about 4km. west of *Swiss Peak*. This is the peak that stands out prominently in the view up the Skeldal, and there is no record of an ascent; however, it is unlikely that a mountain so close to Malmberg has gone unnoticed and unclimbed for so many years. There may also be something worth exploring at the head of the Kishmul Glacier but this is an area of doubtful rock.

It is probable that most of the mountains round the Schuchert and lower half of the Lang have by now been climbed. Higher up the Lang there is scope for exploration in the big glacier between it and the Gannochy. The pass leading over to the Sefstroms Glacier does not seem to have been crossed and there are several peaks east and south-east of *Diadem* of which there are no recorded ascents.

The Dalmore and upper Roslin glaciers seem to have plenty to offer and they give an alternative line of approach to the unclimbed peaks around *Cantabrigia*. There are also several high unclimbed mountains on the east side of the northernmost arm of the Roslin Gletscher, which descends from Newnham Col, but this is one of the most inaccessible parts of the Staunings.

The Spörre and Duart glaciers and the area extending west to the Prinsesse Gletscher have been pretty thoroughly explored by the Swiss and German parties of 1964, 1966 and 1967; the Prinsesse itself probably has little to offer since the attentions of Claude Rey's party in 1968.

The Bjørnbo Gletscher and its many offshoots must still have plenty to offer by way of first ascents, although the Scottish party of 1961 probably got the best. However, there is plenty of scope in the area to the west. The Neptune, Triton, Uranus (Oxford) and Aries glaciers are still largely unexplored from the climbing point of view and a few of the many peaks surrounding them nearly reach eight thousand feet. Clarkson's party in 1961 observed apparently easy passes between the Jupiter and Triton glaciers just south of *Nevis*, and between the Mercury, Uranus and Aries glaciers. These will doubtless prove useful in future exploration.

Finally, west again, is the huge Borgbjerg Gletscher whose mountains, with the exception of the two climbed in 1971, are unexplored. The west side of the Borgbjerg is mainly flat ice-cap, and the most promising areas (judging by aerial photographs and map 71 Ø. 2) are the mountains on the east side of the glacier, and those at its head on the north-east side of the Orion-Borgbjerg col where there appear to be three or four peaks over 2500m. high. These are probably the highest unclimbed mountains in the South Staunings.

Clearly the vast majority of unclimbed mountains in the Staunings Alps is in the south-west, and the best route of approach to them is not from Mesters Vig but from Scoresbysund where there is a small airstrip suitable for light planes. It should be possible to hire an Eskimo boat at Scoresbysund and sail up Scoresby Sound and into Nordvest

Fjord. Thereafter, long but probably fairly easy approaches can be made up the three main glaciers: the Borgbjerg, Neptune and Uranus. At the time of writing, one expedition has already taken this line of approach to the Bjørnbo Gletscher.

Finally, although the list of unclimbed mountains in the Staunings becomes smaller year by year, there is an unlimited scope for hard and direct routes on mountains that so far have been climbed by their easiest or most obvious lines. Naturally most of the climbing done so far in the Staunings has tended to avoid unnecessary difficulties in order to get to the tops of mountains. Now the time has come when, once the 'easy' routes are known, more direct and difficult ascents can be made, and of these there is no shortage. Many superb possibilities come to mind; for example there is the south face of *Dunottar*, three thousand feet of granite slabs and buttresses; the intimidating north face of the *Bersaerkertinde*; the *Dansketinde–Norsketinde* traverse; the north-west ridge of *Bolvaerket*; *Sussex* direct from the Cantabrae by its west ridge. The list is endless. These and many similar climbs will keep climbers busy for years to come.

Nathorsts Land

Nathorsts Land lies to the west of Alpe Fjord and extends for 110 to 130km. westwards to the inland ice-cap. The eastern part, which is easily accessible, is bounded on the north by Forsblads Fjord and on the south by the Furesö. The huge Violin Gletscher, which flows into the western end of the Furesö, more or less separates the eastern part of Nathorsts Land from the inland ice-cap. This eastern part has been frequently visited by scientific and climbing expeditions in the past fifteen years.

In eastern Nathorsts Land the broad and low-lying Schaffhauserdal separates a group of 2000m. mountains in the north-east corner from the extensive ice-cap which occupies most of the rest of the land. The edge of this plateau drops steeply into the Schaffhauserdal, and on the sides facing Alpe Fjord and Dammen the 1800m. plunge of buttresses from the ice-cap to sea-level is even more spectacular.

The Schaffhauserdal is the easiest access route into the eastern part of Nathorsts Land and several glaciers descend from the ice-cap, with steep peaks and buttresses between them. The largest two of these glaciers are the Sydvest Gletscher and the Sand Gletscher, separated by a long ridge terminating at the prominent peak called *Ardvreck*. North of the Sand Gletscher, the cliffs and buttresses of the *Klosterbjerge* tower over the upper part of the Schauffhauserdal. The Sydvest Gletscher provides a fairly easy route up to the ice-cap but the Sand Gletscher seems to be very steep in its upper part and also is separated from the ice-cap by cliffs.

The Nathorsts Land ice-cap, which is bounded on the west by the Violin Gletscher, is about 50km. in extent from east to west and rather less from north to south. It is an undulating plateau whose highest point is about 2400m.; it drops gradually towards the south-east where its edge, overlooking

Dammen, is about 2000m. high. Two steep and narrow glaciers drop from this corner of the ice-cap almost to sea level:
the Trekant Gletscher towards Alpe Fjord and the Smalle
Gletscher towards the Fureső. The rock peaks around the
Trekant are particularly fine.

The mountains in the north-eastern corner of Nathorsts
Land are not as formidable nor as impressive as the Staunings Alps and the highest is a rounded snow dome about
2400m. high. The others are for the most part narrow ridges
of scree and slate-like rock with none of the grand buttresses
and walls of the Staunings Alps. The Galenadal descends
from the centre of this group of mountains to Alpe Fjord,
opposite the Fangshytte Gletscher. The Alpe Fjord shore of
Nathorsts Land between Kap Maechel and the Trekant
Gletscher is fairly flat and gives very pleasant walking in contrast with the opposite shore. Some parties have preferred
this shoreline as a walking route (with ferry connections) to
the head of Alpe Fjord.

Like Scoresby Land, Nathorsts Land had been well explored by the expeditions of Dr Lauge Koch before the arrival of the first climbers in the late nineteen-fifties; huts at
Kap Maechel and at the head of Forsblads Fjord are evi-
dence of much earlier visits by Danish and Norwegian
hunters. It is certain that geologists from Koch's expeditions
made the earliest climbs in Nathorsts Land and reached the
ice-cap.

The 1958 Scottish Expedition made a short visit to Nathorsts Land. The prominent peak (Pt. 1866m.) between the
Sydvest Gletscher and the Sand Gletscher was climbed by its
easy north-east ridge by Paterson, Cameron, Rose and Bennet, who named it Ardvreck. The same party reached the
ice-cap by the Sydvest Gletscher and climbed to the highest
point overlooking Alpe Fjord, from where there was a wonderful view eastwards to the Staunings Alps.

In 1961 members of the Leicester University East Greenland Expedition reached the ice-cap from the head of the
Schaffhauserdal and climbed to its highest point. (Ref. 31.)

In 1968 Graham Tiso's Scottish party visited the Trekant

Gletscher. Tiso and Brian Hill traversed the four-peaked ridge overlooking Alpe Fjord on the north side of the Trekant and terminating in Pt. 1904m.

In 1970 three expeditions made longer visits to Nathorsts Land. The St. Andrews University East Greenland Expedition spent two weeks in the north-east corner and climbed seven peaks in that area, including the highest which they called *The Great Snow Crest*. Their other summits were north-east of this one, at the head of the Galenadal and the Bishop's Glacier. This expedition came to an unfortunate end when Roger Nisbet fell just below the top of a 2000m. peak, as a result of loose rock giving way, and broke his leg. In a thirty-six hour epic two of his companions descended to Alpe Fjord and canoed to Mesters Vig where a helicopter was luckily available for an immediate rescue flight. (Ref. 32.)

The Ladies Scottish Climbing Club, after a visit to the Bersaerkerbrae which included an all-female ascent of the *Bersaerkerspire*, made several climbs from the Schafferhauserdal. These included a second ascent of *Ardvreck*, an ascent of *Pt. 1918m.* on the big snow plateau north of the valley, and the traverse of *Pts. 1850m.* and *1973m.* between the Galenadal and the Schaffhauserdal.

Finally, a German party of four climbers led by Wolfgang Weinzierl climbed seven peaks in the neighbourhood of the Trekant Gletscher. Most of these climbs were mixed rock, snow and ice of quite high standard in what is almost certainly the best corner of Nathorsts Land from the climbers' point of view.

Geology

The Scoresby Peninsula between Kong Oscars Fjord and Scoresby Sound is an area of considerable geological variety.

Jameson Land, forming the bulk of the peninsula, is largely formed of Palaeozoic and Mesozoic sedimentary rocks producing highland of a hilly rather than an alpine character and therefore of limited mountaineering interest. In the south-east, however, a prominent north-south fault divides these sediments from older Caledonian crystalline rocks to form the separate peninsula of Liverpool Land with its rugged and exciting mountainous coastline. In the north, the sediments are interrupted by an intrusion of younger basic igneous rocks which form the Werner Bjerge. These form a massif some 30km wide, reaching a height of about 1800m. and carrying glaciers, but partly composed of dangerously unreliable syenite rock and lacking the dramatic character exhibited by the peaks of the Staunings Alps adjoining the Werner Bjerge to the west.

The Staunings area is divided from the rest of the Scoresby Peninsula by the Skeldal Fault, running north to south from Kong Oscars Fjord to the Schuchert Dal and Scoresby Sound. Virtually the whole region is mountainous and glaciated and is composed of three main categories of rock – ancient Pre-Cambrian to Devonian sediments, 'granitised' sediments or 'older granites', and younger intrusive granites. The relationship between these three elements is fundamental to the geology of the Staunings region.

The Ancient Sediments
These occupy the areas on either side of Alpe Fjord below the Vikingebrae and to the north and north-east of the Staunings Alps proper. They take the form of phyllites, quartzites, mica schists and gneisses. Here the peaks tend to be lower, less dramatic and less attractive than in the igneous areas

further south. There is more scree, slopes are less steep, and the rocks are in general prominently stratified and more variable in quality. Subsequent to the folding which uplifted these rocks, the eruptive forces which produced the Werner Bjerge created dykes of syenite and basalt which cut through this northern sedimentary area. In addition, there are a number of prominent faults here, and in the east the rocks tend to dip downwards to the east.

The Older Granites

During the Caledonian period of mountain building, nearly 500 million years ago, the ancient sediments described above were folded upward and later subjected to replacement and intrusion by the igneous material which today forms the spectacular peaks of the Staunings.

The first phase of this was a complex process by which molten granitic materials assimilated and overwhelmed the sedimentary country rocks. This has resulted in a very heterogeneous type of granitic rock with varying colour, grain size and other features. Sometimes the former sedimentary structures are preserved in the new material and in places the metamorphosed remnants of the ancient sediments survive as enclaves of quartzite, gneiss and similar rocks. In fact much of this first phase produced not granite but 'granitised' sediments.

The Younger Granites

In the late Caledonian period these granites were intruded discordantly through the first phase material and the peripheral untouched sediments. They formed homogeneous, massive granites and granodiorites. Unlike those affected by the earlier phase, the sediments adjacent to and trapped within these newer granites remain largely unaltered. Much of the northern part of the Staunings Alps proper and beyond Alpe Fjord in Nathorsts Land is made up of this younger rock.

A still later phase of intrusion is represented by the bright red granites found in the interior of the massif and often forming colourful patches and veins among other rock.

The result of this geological history is a region of extra-ordinary appeal for mountaineers. The forces of erosion have acted upon these resistant rocks to produce serried ranks of sharp and exciting peaks, flanked by pinnacled arêtes and steep faces or buttresses, and covering a wide range of difficulty. In most places, as a consequence of its igneous or metamorphic character, the rock is sound for rock climbing. Finally, and unusually so in a region with the above qualities, there is a great range of colour, texture and structural form which adds greatly to the pleasure of climbing in the Staunings Alps.

Fauna of Scoresby Land

The following notes have been compiled by the author and are based largely on material in the Dundee University Scoresby Land Expedition Report (Ref. 27) which is the work of Dr Iain Smart. Grateful acknowledgement is made for permission to use this source of information. Any errors in the following notes are due to the author's incorrect interpretation of his learned friend's work.

There are five resident land mammals in Scoresby Land; the musk ox, arctic fox, arctic hare, lemming and ermine. The caribou and polar wolf have only recently become extinct. At sea there are four types of seal, the commonest being the fjord seal, and the polar bear.

The musk ox is probably the most interesting of the mammals as it is seen only in north-east Greenland. It is quite common in Scoresby Land and the population in the Schuchert Dal, which is its stronghold, is between 100 and 200. Much smaller numbers have been seen near Mesters Vig, in the hills behind the airstrip, and along the coastline of Kong Oscars Fjord and Alpe Fjord. It is a large, ponderous animal with thick curved horns and long shaggy wool which is very soft and fine. It should be treated with respect since, although it is normally rather solitary in its habits and moves away at the approach of humans, it may be dangerous at close quarters and can move surprisingly fast. The musk ox is protected on account of its rarity and it is an unforgettable experience to see these strange lonely creatures of the arctic.

The arctic fox is common and is quite likely to come to climbers' camps in search of food. The foxes were hunted until about 15 years ago when fur prices dropped, the trapping being done in winter when the fur is at its best.

The arctic hare remains white all year and is thus rather conspicuous in the summer months. It has been seen in many localities, from the hillside above Dammen to the Schuchert Dal.

The ermine, a small weasel-like creature, changes colour in summer from white to brown; it lives on lemmings and (in early summer) on eggs and young birds as well. It is a fearless and inquisitive animal, darting among the rocks and even, on one occasion in the author's experience, coming right up to sniff the boot of a motionless explorer.

The lemming is a small hamster-like animal whose numbers can vary considerably from year to year. In summer they live in burrows and their winter nests, which are balls of dried grass, can be seen lying on the tundra. The lemmings themselves have not been seen much by expeditions in recent years. They provide the predators such as foxes, ermines, snowy owls and skuas with their staple diet.

Seals are frequently seen in the waters of Kong Oscars Fjord and Alpe Fjord, and are shot by the Danes at Mesters Vig. The Polar bear is fortunately encountered infrequently. It lives and hunts on the pack ice and seldom comes ashore unless the pack ice itself drifts close inshore.

Some twenty species of birds are commonly seen in Scoresby Land and about half a dozen others are occasionally encountered. Four are year-round residents: the North Greenland rock ptarmigan, Hornemann's redpoll, northern raven and snowy owl. The remainder are summer migrants, most of which breed in the area.

Of the waders that are seen in Europe, the ringed plover, turnstone, sanderling and dunlin are quite commonly seen around Mesters Vig. The grey phalarope and knot are less common. The ringed plover haunts the gravelly flats of the Skeldal and Gefion Pass. Turnstone have been seen along the sandy shore of Kong Oscars Fjord and on the tundra close to the airstrip. Sanderlings have been seen in the Schuchert Dal and dunlin near Festers Vig. The latter were quite unafraid (or unwary) and allowed a close approach.

Skuas, both arctic and long-tailed, are often seen around

Mesters Vig where they can supplement their natural diet of lemmings with scraps of garbage.

The glaucous gull and arctic tern are both common along the coastal regions and up the fiords. They are often to be seen in large numbers at river mouths and glacier outflows. Both breed in large numbers on the Menanders Islands.

The gyr-falcon, snowy owl and northern raven have all been seen in the neighbourhood of Mesters Vig.

Of the small birds, the snow bunting and Greenland wheatear are common and have been seen in many different places, for example the head of Alpe Fjord, Mesters Vig and the Schuchert Dal. Hornemann's redpoll is less common but it has been seen as high as 900m. on rocks and sparse vegetation at the edge of the Sefstroms Glacier.

Of the geese, the pink-footed and barnacle are often seen near Mesters Vig and also in the Schuchert Dal and along the shores of Kong Oscars Fjord. They are known to breed in the gorge of the Tunnelelv, a few miles above Mesters Vig, and at the end of August flocks of over a hundred have been seen on the sandy flats north of Mesters Vig.

The red-throated diver is very widespread in Greenland and is frequently seen and heard along the shores of Kong Oscars Fjord and Alpe Fjord. The great northern diver is less common as Scoresby Land is just about the northern-most limit of its breeding range.

The long-tailed duck and arctic eider are quite common along the Kong Oscars Fjord coast where they have been seen in small flocks. The red-breasted merganser is not so common and is usually seen only in small numbers.

The ptarmigans are remarkably tame and are often seen in the tundra. Their change of plumage to winter all-white occurs about the end of August, some time before the winter snows, and they are then conspicuous in the tundra and among the rocks.

MAMMALS BREEDING IN AND AROUND SCORESBY LAND

Arctic fox	Alopex Lagopus
Arctic hare	Lepus Groenlandicus
Ermine	Mustela Erminea
Lemming	Dicrostonyx Groenlandicus
Musk ox	Ovibos Moschatus
Polar bear	Ursus Maritimus
Bearded seal	Phoca Barbatus
Fjord seal	Phoca Vitulina
Harp seal	Phoca Groenlandica
Ringed seal	Phoca Hispida

Mammals recently become extinct

Caribou	Rangifer Tarandus
Polar wolf	Canis Lupus

BIRDS SEEN IN SCORESBY LAND

Resident:

Hornemann's redpoll	Carduelis Flammea Hornemanni
Northern raven	Corvus Corax Principalis
North Greenland rock ptarmigan	Lagopus Mutus Captus
Snowy owl	Nyctea Scandiaca

Migrant:

Arctic eider	Somateria Mollissima Borealis
Arctic skua	Stercorarious Parasiticus
Arctic tern	Sterna Paradisaea
Barnacle goose	Branta Leucopsis
Dunlin	Calidris Alpina Arctica
Fulmar	Fulmaris Glacialis
Glaucous gull	Larus Hyperboreus
Great northern diver	Gavia Immer
Greenland redpoll	Carduelis Flammea Rostrata
Greenland wheater	Oenanthe Oenanthe Leucorrhoa

Grey phalarope	Phalaropus Fulicarius
Gyr-falcon	Falco Rusticulus
Knot	Calidris Canutus
Long-tailed duck	Clangula Liemalis
Long-tailed skua	Stercorarius Longicaudatus
Meadow pipit	Anthus Pratensis
Pink-footed goose	Anser Fabalis Brachyrhynchus
Red-breasted merganser	Mergus Serrator
Red-throated diver	Gavia Stellata
Ringed plover	Charadrius Liaticula Tundrae
Sabines gull	Xema Sabini
Sanderling	Crocethia Alba
Snow bunting	Plectrophenax Nivalis
Turnstone	Arenaria Interpres

Flora of Scoresby Land

First impressions of Mesters Vig and its surrounding hill-sides, gained as one's aircraft slowly loses height to land, are of a country that is remarkably barren and devoid of any vegetation. At first sight the part of the landscape that is not covered with snow and ice seems to be covered by rock, screes and gravel. At closer acquaintance, however, the flat country surrounding the airstrip, and indeed much of the low lying land is found to have a surprisingly rich plant cover.

The most prolific plant is the heath cassiope tetragona which covers much of the tundra. It has tiny white bell-like flowers, and the leaves dry to a dull brown as the summer progresses. Mixed with the cassiope on the lower hillsides and along the fiord-shores are dwarf willow with its white feathery catkins, dwarf birch (betula nana), crowberry (empetrum nigrum), black bearberry (arctous alpinus) and blaeberry (vaccinium uliginosum). In places these shrubs form a dense covering whose leaves change colour in late summer and create a wonderful and vivid pattern of colours, red, yellow and gold. In addition the blaeberries are sweet and succulent to eat.

Of the many flowers that grow on the tundra, higher up among rocks and screes, and even on the high mountains, mention may be made of only a few. On the tundra the yellow arctic poppy (papaver radicatum), mountain aven (dryas octopetala) and the purple arctic willowherb (chamaenerion latifolium) are the most colourful of the common flowers.

Higher up on rocky hillsides and among scree many plants manage to thrive. Among them are the flowers already mentioned as well as harebell (campanula rotundifolia), alpine mouse-ear chickweed (cerastium alpinum), and mountain sorrel (oxyria dygna). The green leaves of the latter are very pleasant to eat, and may well provide the climber with his only natural source of Vitamin C in Greenland.

Many saxifrages are to be found, of which the most common are probably the yellow mountain saxifrage (sax. aizoides) which thrives in moist places, and the purple saxifrage (sax. oppositifolia). Drooping saxifrage (sax. cernua) and saxifraga caespitosa thrive in the stoniest of terrains. Saxifraga Nathorstii, which is also found, is peculiar to this part of Greenland. The moss campion (silene acaulis) is found commonly, as in Europe, high up in the mountains nestling on ledges and in rocky corners.

These are just a few of the many flowers and shrubs that will delight the eye of the naturalist. Far from being an arctic waste as many people imagine, the coast-line and lower hills of Scoresby Land are carpeted with flowers, shrubs and heath which spring up as the snow melts in June and the sun warms the moist earth. For a month or two they flourish and towards the end of August a blaze of colour marks the end of summer. By September the icy winds blow from the north and soon the Arctic Riveria becomes a desolate white wilderness under a sunless sky.

Information for Expedition Planning

1. TRAVEL

The information in this chapter is intended to be of use to parties in the preliminary stages of planning an expedition to the Staunings Alps. Some of this information is liable to become outdated or otherwise altered, and while it is correct at the time of writing it is quite possible that some changes, particularly in charter prices, will occur.

The first step to be taken by any party intending to go to Greenland is to contact the Danish Embassy in their country to obtain the regulations currently in existence for parties going to Greenland, and then to make a formal application for permission to the Greenland Ministry of the Danish Government. (Permission at this stage does not include permission to land at Mesters Vig which must be sought separately.)

Maps and aerial photographs of the Staunings Alps can be purchased from the Geodetic Institute, Copenhagen. The most recent maps seem to be numbers 72 Ø 2 (Scale 1 : 250,000) for the northern half, and 71 Ø 2 (Scale 1 : 200,000) for the southern half. Map 72 Ø 2 is rather out of date and inaccurate, and may by now be superseded. Aerial photographs are particularly useful as they are much more detailed and accurate than maps – so much so that the element of uncertainty inherent in mountain exploration is to some extent reduced by the time one has studied aerial photographs of a particular area.

Travel arrangements to and from Greenland are one of the most important single items of planning. As there are no scheduled air services to Mesters Vig, the last stage of the journey must be by charter flight. In the interests of economy the length of the charter flight should be as short as possible, so most parties go to Iceland by scheduled flight and from there to Greenland by charter flight. There is how-

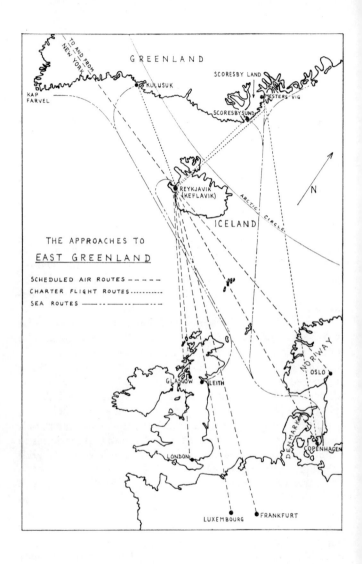

THE APPROACHES TO
EAST GREENLAND

SCHEDULED AIR ROUTES — — —
CHARTER FLIGHT ROUTES ....
SEA ROUTES — ·· — ·· — ··—

GREENLAND

TO AND FROM
NEW YORK

KULUSUK

KAP
FARVEL

SCORESBY LAND

MESTERS · VIG

SCORESBYSUND

REYKJAVIK
(KEFLAVIK)

ICELAND

ARCTIC CIRCLE

N

NORWAY

OSLO

GLASGOW

LEITH

DENMARK

COPENHAGEN

LONDON

LUXEMBOURG

FRANKFURT

ever no reason except cost why parties should not fly from Copenhagen, Glasgow or elsewhere by charter flight all the way.

However, as just mentioned, most parties fly to Keflavik or Reykjavik by scheduled flight, and onwards from Reykjavik to Mesters Vig by charter flight. There are direct flights to Reykjavik (or Keflavik) from Copenhagen, Glasgow, London, Oslo, Frankfurt, Luxemburg and New York.

The most experienced charter flight operator between Reykjavik and Mesters Vig is Icelandair, and it can offer a variety of aircraft. The following prices and payloads apply at the time of writing for a single flight from Reykjavik to Mesters Vig and back:

Aircraft	Payload	Price
DC 6B	6450kg	£1570
Fokker Friendship	3500kg	£1200
DC 3	1600kg	£900
Bonanza	270kg	£270

The advantage of chartering a large aircraft on the basis of cost per kilogramme is obvious.

Stirling Airways of Copenhagen can also offer non-stop charter flights from Copenhagen to Mesters Vig.

The charter flight company will make the necessary official approach to the Danish Civil Aviation Authority for permission to land at Mesters Vig.

The journey to Reykjavik may also be made by sea on the m.v. *Gullfoss* (Icelandic Steamship Company) which sails about once every ten days from Leith (Edinburgh).

Freight can be sent to Iceland by air or sea, the latter being of course cheaper although, if the quantity of freight is large enough, the air freight rate may not be prohibitively expensive. Sea freight will normally go to Iceland in the m.v. *Gullfoss*. It is also possible to send freight directly to Greenland from Copenhagen; the agents for these services are Kongelige Gronlands Handel of Copenhagen. To ensure arrival in time such freight should be sent a year in advance.

Once permission has been granted to fly in to Mesters Vig, contact should be made with the Station Manager there to inform him of one's plans. While all parties must be self-supporting in every respect and cannot expect to receive any goods or services at Mesters Vig, it is possible that certain items such as petrol or paraffin may be obtainable by prior arrangement. It may also be possible to arrange with the Station Manager for the hire of one of the trucks at Mesters Vig for conveying equipment, either up to the old mine in Tunnelelv or down to the harbour, and for the hire of the motor launch normally used by the staff at Mesters Vig for hunting trips in Kong Oscars Fjord.

It is also possible to enquire from the Station Manager as to whether any companies (such as Nordisk Mineselskab) operating in the area may have a helicopter for hire. The use of a helicopter greatly reduces the effort of carrying a lot of food and equipment into the mountains but the cost is considerable (about £200 per hour) and the availability always depends on the prior demands of company operations.

One important matter that requires attention is insurance. The Greenland Ministry insist that insurance cover is taken out against the cost of possible search and rescue in Greenland and a specially chartered rescue flight to Reykjavik. The sum to be insured against is currently £1200 per person in any party and the premium in the U.K. is about £1 per person per week in Greenland.

Parties going to the Staunings Alps will do well to get in touch with Exploration and Travel Limited, a small travel agency which specialises in organising and coordinating parties to mountainous and other remote parts of the world. Exploration and Travel may be of assistance in putting small parties in touch with each other to enable them to share charter flights, or in acting as a clearing house for information, and they may also be able to arrange suitable insurance cover.

The matter of equipment and food planning poses no particular problems except that, in order to make charter flight payload calculations at an early stage, it is necessary to estimate accurately the total load of persons, food and equipment in a party. Food and equipment lists should be as economical as possible in terms of weight to reduce transport costs. The list at the end of this chapter is given as an example of the amount of food and equipment, and its weight, that might be required by a party of six for a four week expedition to the head of Alpe Fjord.

List of useful addresses:

Ministry for Greenland, Hausegade 3, Copenhagen K, Denmark.

Geodetic Institute, Rigsdagsgarden 7, Copenhagen K., Denmark.

Kongelige Gronlands Handel, Strandgade, Copenhagen K., Denmark.

Icelandic Steamship Company. Agents in Great Britain: Currie Line Limited, 16 Bernard Street, Leith, Edinburgh 6.

MacGregor, Gow and Holland Limited, 16 St Helen's Place, London.

Icelandair Offices in Great Britain: 94 Queen Street, Glasgow; 73 Grosvenor Street, London, W.1.

Stirling Airways, Kastrup Airport, Copenhagen, Denmark.

Exploration and Travel Limited, 1100 Pollokshaws Road, Glasgow, S.1., Great Britain.

2. WEATHER

As has been stated previously, the weather in July and August – the best season for climbing – can usually be relied on to be warm and settled; this is particularly true in the northern part of Scoresby Land. The prevailing wind in July on the East Greenland coast is from the north, and is quite light. The east wind when it blows tends to bring mist, low clouds and rain in from the sea. Although winds are normally light, local land features such as narrow, enclosed fiords can produce high winds locally. Katabatic winds blow down from the ice-cap towards the sea, and where they are channelled by land features such as big glaciers flowing from the ice-cap down to the sea or long fiords penetrating towards the ice-cap katabatic winds can be very strong. Furesö and the head of Alpe Fjord are examples of places where katabatic winds are quite likely, and wind speeds of 30 knots (about 55km. per hour) have been experienced at sea level, while a few hundred metres up the hillside above the fiord calm conditions prevailed.

Severe blizzards with high winds, driving snow and very low temperatures are quite rare in the Staunings Alps in summer. Bad weather is more likely to involve low cloud or mist, light winds and snowfall (rain at sea-level). These conditions can persist for a few days (seldom more) and may make climbing and high level travel very difficult, but they are not likely to be dangerous to a competent party with adequate reserves of food. There is no instance known to the author of a climbing party in the Staunings Alps in summer being placed in serious danger or difficulty by a bad storm.

Temperatures in July and August are not extreme, although mid-day temperatures in July can be unexpectedly warm, up to 70 to 75°F (22 to 25°C). During cold spells temperatures at glacier level are seldom less than about 23°F (minus 5°C), and summit temperatures about 14°F (minus 10°C); these temperatures might be encountered in late August at night or during sunless weather.

Thus no special precautions against frostbite are necessary beyond those which any competent party would take when climbing snow-covered mountains.

3. EQUIPMENT

Three factors influence the choice of equipment for a small expedition to the Staunings Alps. First, everything must be flown in to Mesters Vig at high air freight rates; second, once in Greenland everything must be carried into the mountains on the climbers' backs; and third, the weather is in general reliably good and warm. Large expeditions might have an air-drop of supplies into the mountains, but, once again, the question of weight would be all-important.

The following notes are therefore written from the view-point of a small expedition aiming to reduce weight to a minimum and to avoid the unnecessary expense of too-specialised equipment or high air freight charges.

Boat: An expedition wanting its own boat for travel to and from Alpe Fjord will almost certainly have to settle for an inflatable rubber dingy. A 10- to 12-ft. (3–4m.) dingy is about the smallest that is practicable; a dingy with a rigid wooden transom is preferable to a dingy with an inflated stern as the latter tends to float lower in the water at the stern when an outboard motor is mounted. (For example, to take the Avon range of inflatable dingies, the Red Rover Mk III is better than the Redshank in this respect.)

Outboard Motor: A reliable outboard motor is essential as a breakdown may have very unpleasant consequences. It may be desirable in the case of certain types of motor (e.g. Sea-gull) to modify the air intake to prevent water entering the engine in heavy weather for, when the motor is mounted on an inflatable dingy, the air intake may be only about eight-een inches above the water.

Anyone using an inflatable dingy and outboard motor for the first time should familiarise himself with the handling characteristics, fuel consumption and payload before leaving for the arctic.

Canoes: Several expeditions in recent years have used canoes for travelling round the coast from Mesters Vig to Alpe Fjord. They do not have the same load carrying capacity as a rubber dingy, but they may have their uses and are doubt-less faster than walking round the rough parts of the coast.

Sledges: Some expeditions have used sledges to haul food and equipment up easy glaciers, but it is doubtful if a small party can justify taking a large sledge which may weigh about 40lb (18kg.); even large parties have found them of doubtful value. Some climbers have experimented with chil-drens' polythene sledges which are very light and can be used for hauling single heavy sacs (60 to 80lbs, 25 to 35kg) along easy glaciers. With a little ingenuity the polythene sledge can be fitted with shoulder straps and used as a pack frame when sledge hauling is not possible. It would be well to experiment with this rather unconventional form of load carrying before committing oneself in the Staunings Alps.

Skis: In July the large amount of soft snow on the glaciers makes the use of skis advantageous though not absolutely necessary for glacier travel. In August the need for skis is less. Generally most of the main glaciers are fairly level and easy and a high standard of downhill skiing is not necessary. The main use of skis is likely to be on those glaciers where ski-walking would be the most apt way to describe progress, both uphill and downhill. Light Scandinavian touring skis weigh 2½ to 3lb (about 1.25kg.) per pair but the addition of bindings will probably double this weight. Ski sticks (which should be longer than those normally used for downhill skiing) can also be used as tent poles. Skins are necessary for steep uphill skiing and are probably worth taking; special ski waxes are a lighter alternative for those familiar with their use.

Tents: There are now several very lightweight tents and flysheets available; a 7lb (3.25kg) lightweight tent is greatly preferable to a 15lb (6.75kg) conventional 2–3 man tent but is unfortunately much more expensive. (The price of mountain tents appears to be inversely proportional to their weight.) In settled weather the use of tents at campsites on tundra or moraine is not absolutely necessary because quite adequate protection can be given by a flysheet or large groundsheet. It is probably a justifiable risk not to use flysheets on conventional tents at high altitude in order to save weight.

Ice Axes: Short ice axes of the type now popular for steep ice climbs are useless for glacier travel and probing for crevasses. Long ice axes (30–32 ins.) (75–80cm.) are preferable for all-round use. Alternatively one (or two) ski sticks can be used for glacier travel and crevasse probing, with the short ice axe kept for steep climbing.

Crampons: A good quality, lightweight, 12-point pair of crampons must be regarded as essential.

Ropes: Conventional climbing rope is perfectly suitable. Fixed ropes have not hitherto been used for climbs in the Staunings Alps but, bearing in mind that one may frequently have to descend quite hard climbs, long ropes (200 to 300ft., 60–90m.) for abseiling are an advantage. Slings or harnesses to facilitate crevasse rescue should not be forgotten.

Pitons: Up to the present there have been very few climbs done in the Staunings which have involved continuously high standard or artificial climbing. The time is probably not far distant, however, when attempts will be made on big steep walls and these will entail the logistic problems of carrying up food, ropes and equipment for multi-day climbs. On the other hand most climbers in the Staunings Alps will continue to climb and explore medium grade routes, and for weight carrying reasons the use of pitons, fixed ropes and other aids will be kept to a minimum. Ice pitons are probably more useful than rock pitons, and 'deadman' belays can (in addition to their primary function) be used with a suitable ice axe attachment as snow shovels.

Boots: Bearing in mind that one is likely to do more walking than climbing in the Staunings Alps, a comfortable pair of boots with not-too-rigid soles is preferable to very rigid rock climbing boots. Of greater importance, however, boots should be of very good quality as they will be subjected to exceptionally rough wear. Ideally boots should be nearly new and properly broken in before going to the Staunings.

Clothing: No special clothing is required; clothes suitable for Britain or the European Alps are adequate for the Staunings. Climbing helmets, knee length gaiters and lightweight cagoules are all very desirable. Good snow-goggles are necessary and a light, broad-brimmed cotton hat (cricketer's fielding-out hat) gives good protection against the fierce glare of the mid-day sun. A single good quality sleeping bag is adequate, even at high altitude, and an air-mattress (plus puncture repair outfit) provides the necessary insulation and comfort on stony and icy camp sites.

Cooking Equipment, etc: For cooking, the Primus (or similar) stove is still the best, and together with its paraffin fuel it has a better 'heat output to weight' ratio than Butane gas cookers. Conventional aluminium billy cans are quite adequate, and pressure cookers are not necessary. (This may not be the case in a large party with large quantities of dehydrated vegetables to cook). Polythene carriers for water and paraffin are necessary, but it may be an advantage to use cheap ones which can be discarded at the end of an expedition.

Miscellaneous: Mosquitoes may be very troublesome at low altitude campsites, particularly during July. (In August the first frosts soon get rid of them). A good mosquito repellant is therefore necessary. The author has found 'Moon Tiger', an incense which is burned slowly in one's tent, very effective for keeping mosquitoes out.

Flares or rockets may be considered for signalling or use in emergency but it should be remembered that flares are not easily seen at a long distance unless it is dark, which is never the case in the Staunings in July or August.

It may be possible by prior arrangement with the Station Manager at Mesters Vig to obtain paraffin and petrol there. Otherwise these items will have to be flown in.

4. FOOD

Neither the terrain nor the climatic conditions make it necessary to have special polar rations. The normal type of balanced and varied diet as used on most mountaineering expeditions is perfectly adequate for the Staunings Alps; a calorific value of 3500–4000 kcals. should be sufficient. One of the more important factors to consider is weight: every item of food must be air-freighted, every item must be carried on one's back. Dehydrated foods are valuable on account of their lightness; foods should be easy and quick to prepare for paraffin, too, is rationed. Ideally, rations should be packed in man-day boxes before going to Greenland.

Specimen Food and Equipment List

SIX PEOPLE FOR FOUR WEEKS

Item	*Weight*		*Notes*
	lb.	kg.	
Food and Packing	480	218	Based on 2·75lb (1·25kg.) per man-day plus 18lb (8kg.) for packing.
Tents	60	27	Two 3-man mountain tents, one larger tent for base camp.
Rope	40	18	Three 240ft. ropes (220m. total).
Pitons, karabiners, slings	40	18	
12ft. Inflatable Dingy	65	30	Complete with pumps, oars repair kit.
5h.p. Outboard Motor	45	20	Complete with tools, filler funnel, spare plugs and other minor parts.
Lifejackets, 2.	5	2	
Petrol, 20 gallons (90 litres)	150	68	Based on two return trips to head of Alpe Fjord, 300 miles at 15 miles per gallon (480km. at 5.4km./litre).
Oil, 2 gallons (9 litres)	15	7	Based on motor using 10:1 petrol – oil mixture.
Cooking pots, Utensils, etc.	10	5	
Primus Stoves, 4.	10	5	
Paraffin, 7 gallons (32 litres)	50	22	Based on one third of a pint per man-day (19 centilitres).
Jerrycans and bottles for petrol and paraffin	10	5	
Skis, ski sticks, 4 pairs.	20	9	Lightweight Norwegian skis with Kandahar bindings.

Specimen Food and Equipment List

Item	Weight		Notes
	lb.	kg.	
Flares, rockets.	10	5	For emergency and signalling.
Medical supplies.	20	9	
Ice Axes, 8.	20	9	Two spare for emergency.
Crampons, 7 pairs.	10	5	One spare pair for emergency.
Personal clothing, Sleeping Bag, Air matress, Rucksack, Knife, Fork, Spoon, Plate, Mug.	240	108	Based on 40lb. (18kg.) per man.
	————		
TOTAL	1300lb.	590 kg.	

Add the weight of six people fully clothed to obtain the total weight on the outward flight. The weight on the return flight is reduced by (at least) the weight of food, petrol, oil, paraffin and any other expendable items.

Explanatory Notes

Danish words used in nomenclature:

Bjerg	..	Mountain	
Brae	..	Gletscher	.. Glacier
Dal	..	Valley	
Fjeld	..	Hill, fell	
Kap	..	Cape, headland	
Passet	..	Col, pass	
Spids	..	Point, summit	
Tinde	..	Peak, summit	

Standards or grades of climbing difficulty:

Individual Pitches			Overall		
I	..	Moderate	F	..	Facile (Easy)
II	..	Difficult	PD	..	Peu difficile (Barely Difficult)
III	..	Very Difficult	AD	..	Assez difficile (Quite Difficult)
IV	..	Severe	D	..	Difficile (Difficult)
V	..	Very Severe	TD	..	Très difficile (Very Difficult)
VI	..	Hard Very Severe	ED	..	Extrêmement difficile (Extremely Difficult)

Other abbreviations used:

N .. North	S .. South	W .. West	E .. East
NW .. North-west	S.S.E. .. South-south-east, etc.		
hp. .. horse-power	m.v. .. motor vessel		

Metric Conversions:

1 metre (m.)	=	3·281 feet (ft.)
1000m.	=	3281ft.
2000m.	=	6562ft.
3000m.	=	9843ft.

Explanatory Notes

1 kilometre (km.)	=	0·621 miles		
1·609km.	=	1 mile		
100 grammes (gm.)	=	3·5 ounces (oz.) Avoirdupois		
454gm.	=	1 pound (lb.)		
1 kilogramme (kg.)	=	2·2lbs.		
0·567 litres	=	1 pint (pt).	=	0·125 gallons (gal)
1 litre	=	1·76pt	=	0·22gal.
4·5 litres	=	8pt	=	1gal.
1 Imperial gallon	=	1·2 U.S. gallons		

Bibliography

The numbers given below relate to the references quoted in the text.

1. *The Mountain World*, 1953. (Swiss Foundation for Alpine Research.) Pp. 189–195, 'Summer Climbs in the Staunings Range' by Peter Braun.

2. *The Mountain World*, 1962/63. (S.F.A.R.). Pp. 161–186, 'The Stauning Alps of Eastern Greenland' by Malcolm Slesser. Pp. 187–196, 'The South Stauning Alps in 1961' by James Clarkson.

3. *The Mountain World*, 1966/67. (S.F.A.R.). Pp. 113–127, 'Climbing in the Arctic. The German Greenland Expedition in the Staunings Alps 1966' by Karl M. Herrligkoffer. Pp. 128–145. 'Mountaineering in Greenland 1870–1966' by Erik Hoff.

4. *The Mountain World*, 1968/69. (S.F.A.R.). Pp. 146–152, 'Eighteen Years Climbing in the Stauning Alps' by D. J. Bennet. Pp. 185–188, 'A short list of Expeditions and Climbs in the Staunings Alps' by D. J. Bennet.

4. *Arctic Riviera* by E. Hofer. (Kümmerly & Frey, Berne), 1957.

6. *Spedizione d'Alpinismo in Groenlandia* by Guido Monzino. (Mondadori, Verona), 1966.

7. *Montagne di Groenlandia* by Mario Fantin. (Tamari Editori, Bologna), 1969.

8. *Norsk Polar Tidende*, Nos. 1–3, p. 4 and Nos. 4–6, p. 25, 1952.

9. *Norsk Fjellsport*. (Oslo), 1958.

10. *Meddelelser om Grönland*, 154, No. 3, 1958. (Copenhagen.)

Bibliography

11. *Meddelelser om Grönland,* 153, No. 4, 1958. (Copenhagen.)

12. *La Montagne et Alpinisme,* February 1956. (French Alpine Club).

13. *Ö. A. V. Yearbook,* 1958. (Austrian Alpine Club.)

14. *Die Alpen,* 1958, (Swiss Alpine Club.)

15. *Scottish Mountaineering Club Journal,* Vol. 26, No. 150, 1959.

16. *Scottish Mountaineering Club Journal,* Vol. 27, No. 152, 1961.

17. *Scottish Mountaineering Club Journal,* Vol. 27, No. 153, 1962.

18. *The Alpine Journal,* Vol. 66, No. 303, 1961. Pp. 250–260, '1960 Greenland Expedition' by J. A. Jackson, A. Blackshaw and I. McNaught-Davis.

19. *The Alpine Journal,* Vol. 69, No. 309, 1964. Pp. 253–258, 'Imperial College East Greenland Expedition, 1963' by H. D. D. Watson.

20. *Cambridge East Greenland Expedition,* 1963. General Report.

21. *Cambridge Mountaineering Club Journal,* 1964.

22. *Die Alpen.* 1964, p. 191. (S.A.C.)

23. *Die Alpen,* 1965, (S.A.C.). Pp. 225–232, 'Groenland' by Paul Meinherz.

24. *Akademischer Alpen-Club Zürich, Yearbook* No. 68/69, 1963–64.

25. *Der Bergkamerad,* 28th Year. Vol. 4, p. 173.

26. *Queen Mary College East Greenland Expedition Report,* 1968. (Queen Mary College Library, London.)

27. *Dundee University Scoresby Land Expedition Report,* 1968. (Dundee University Library.)

28. *Scottish Mountaineering Club Journal,* Vol. 29, No. 160, 1969.

29. *Internationale Nordost Grönland Expedition,* 1968. (Report in German published and circulated privately by Hermann Huber, Munich.)

30. *Expédition Française au Groenland Nord-Est,* 1968. (Report in French published and circulated privately by Claude Rey.)

31. *Leicester University East Greenland Expedition Report.*

32. *St. Andrews 1970 East Greenland Expedition General Report*; edited by R. M. Nisbet.

33. *The Flora of Greenland* by T. W. Blocher, K. Holmen and K. H. K. Jakobsen. (Haasa, Copenhagen and Hurst & Co., London.) 1968.

34. *Birds of Greenland* by F. Salomonsen. 3 volumes. (Munksgaard, Copenhagen.)

35. *The Sledge Patrol* by D. Howarth. (Collins, Edinburgh) 1957. Also Fontana paperback, 1959.

36. *Animals of the Arctic* by Bernard Stonehouse. Ecology of the Far North. (Ward Lock, London). 1971.

INDEX OF PLACE NAMES IN GREENLAND

Page numbers in heavy type refer to the lists of mountains and passes

Achnacarry **58**
Albert 53, **77**
Alpe Fjord 9–15, 22–27, 35–40, 45, 49, 50, 52, 86–94
Angmagssalik 32
Arcturus Gletscher 24
Ardvreck 86–88
Aries Glacier 52, 53, 84
Attilaborgen 15, 19, 37, 43, **65**, 83
Augsburger Spids **70**
Barenzahne **68**
Bastille **61**
Bavariaspids 35, **56**
Beaufort 37, **58**
Beaumaris 48, **59**
Bellevue 23
Berchtesgadener Gletscher (see Hecate Glacier)
Berchtesgadener Kopf **71**
Berchtesgadener Tinde **70**
Berggeistspids **70**
Bersaerkerbrae 13, 14, 16, 19, 22, 23, 36–44, 47, 48, 51, 52, 82, 88
Bersaerkerspire 39, 52, **59**, 82, 88
Bersaerkerspire (West Peak) **76**
Bersaerkertinde 19, 37, 48, **73**, 82, 85
Berzelius Bjerge 26
Bishop's Glacier 88
Bjørnbo Gletscher 13, 17, 18, 20, 39, 40, 52, 53, 84, 85
Blackwall **66**
Black Twin 50, **72**
Blair **63**

Bolvaerket 15, 17, 19, 42, **65**, 82, 85
Bonarbjerg 49, **73**
Borgbjerg Gletscher 10, 13, 16, 18, 20, 46, 51, 53, 84, 85
Bosigran **73**
Bow **66**
Caerleon 38, 44
Caerleon Glacier 38, 44
Caius **65**
Cantabrae 15, 17, 19, 42, 49, 83, 85
Cantabrigia 15, 19, 42, **66**, 83, 84
Carrick **58**
Castle **66**
Castor **70**
Castor Glacier 16, 47
Cavendish Glacier 15, 42, 82
Cerberus **68**
C. F. Knox Tinde (see Knox-tinde)
Christinabjerg 50, **72**
Churchill Col 17, 43, 51, **79**, 83
Cima Est 45, **67**
Cima Ouest 45, **67**
Cirque d'Acropole **75**
Citadel 40, **62**
Clare **65**
Claverhouse **73**
Clavering Island 32
Col de Furesö 51, **81**
Col de Scoresby 51, **81**
Col Major 13–19, 37–39, 42, 47, 48, 51, 52, 54, **79**
Combe d'Argent **75**
Concordia 18, 20, 39, 40, 47

Courier Pass   17, 49, **79**
Crescent Col   15, 17, 41, **79**, 83
Culross   **62**
Daedalus   **62**
Dalmore Glacier   17, 49, 84
Dammen   16, 19, 26, 27, 34–50, 86, 87, 93
Dansketinde   9, 14, 18, 35, 45, 48, **56**, 82, 85
Danmarks Havn   32
Darien   46, **62**
Darien Pass   **80**
Deltadal   23
Diadem   20, 35, 42, 50, **56**, 83
Dinosaur   **62**
Dollar   **62**
Dome   49, **73**
Dôme du Blizzard   51, **75**
Dôme de l'Envoi   **75**
Dôme du Léopard   **75**
Dôme des Séracs   **75**
Dôme du Trappeur   **75**
Donnau Passet   **80**
Downingfjeld   20, 42, **64**, 83
Dreikant   35, **56**, 83
Dreverspitz   49, **73**
Duart Glacier   16, 17, 46, 84
Duart-Roslin Col   **79**
Dudhope   **73**
Dunottar   13, 37, 47, 51, **58**, 85
Dunottar Glacier   13, 36, 37
Dunvegan   36, **57**
Eckhorn   35, **56**
Edinbrae   16, 44, 50, 83
Edinburgh   **62**
Eilan Donan   **58**
Elephant   **66**
Elizabethtinde   34, **55**
Ella Island   32
Elsinore   **59**
Emmanuel   42, **64,** 83
False Col   48, **80**
Fangshytte Gletscher   14, 26, 52, 87
First Point of Aries   **62**
Forsblads Fjord   86, 87

Friheds Gletscher   43
Friheds Pass   14, 34, 43, 50, **78**
Frihedstinde   14, 18, 34, **55**, 82
Furesö   13, 16, 27, 35, 86, 87
Fussener Ryggen   **70**
Galenadal   87, 88
Gannochy Glacier   13, 17, 49, 83
Garmischer Spids   **70**
Gauche Peak   **61**
Gefion Pass   22, 23, 40, **78**, 93
Girton   **66**
Glacier des Oubliettes   51, 75
Glacier des Tours   51
Glacier des Violettes   75
Glamis   19, 36, 44, 47, 48, **57**
Glamis Col   16, 19, 36, 44, 47, **78**
Glatze   **71**
Gonville   **65**
Grandes Jorasses (see Knoxtinde)
Granit Spids   **70**
Grantabrae   15, 35, 36, 42, 50
Grantalang Col   15, **79**
Great Snow Crest   88
Grosse Sidney Gletscher (see Castor Glacier)
Gully Gletscher   13–19, 26, 35–44, 48, 50, 52, 82
Gully-Lang Col   **80**
Hamna Hut   23
Harlech   **59**
Harlech Glacier   44
Hecate Glacier   16, 47
Hellefjeld   **56**
Helmspitzen   45, **68**
Helvedes Pass   34, 53, **80**
Hermann von Barth Tinde   **71**
Hermes   **62**
Hermitage   **61**
Hirschbichler Spids   **71**
Hjornespids   18, 39, 48, **60**
Hochstetter's Forland   33
Hogspids   50, **72**
Holger Danskes Briller   52

Homerton **65**
Inverarnan 38, **59**
Invertebrae 15, 34, 43
Ivar Baardson Gletscher (see Roslin Gletscher)
Jameson Land 9, 89
Jupiter Glacier 18, 39, 40, 84
Kapelle 35, 37, **57**
Kap Maechel 87
Kap Petersen 10, 13, 14, 22, 24, 25, 34, 45
Kap Tobin 10
Karabiner 52, 53, **60**
Kastenberg 15, 35, 45, **57**, 83
Kathispids 33, **55**
Kederbacher Spids **72**
Kemptner Horn **70**
Kensington 44, 47, 48, 51, **67**, 82
Kieferner Toppen **69**
Kilroy **61**
Kilvrough **60**
Kings Peak **64**
Kirkbrae 17, 35, 43, 50
Kirriemuir **63**
Kishmul 19, 44, **67**
Kishmul Glacier 16, 36, 44, 47, 83
Kleine Sidney Gletscher (see Pollux Glacier)
Klosterbjerge 86
Knacke Gletscher 45
Knoxtinde 19, 43, 44, **63**
Kocheler Spids **70**
Kolossen 23
Kong Oscars Fjord 9, 10, 25, 37, 43, 45, 50, 89, 92–94
Korsspids 15, 19, 36, 43, 45, **65**, 82, 83
Krabbe Gletscher 15, 43, 83
L'Acropole **75**
Lambeth 44, 48, **66**
Lamorna **73**
Lancaster 53, **77**
Lang Gletscher 13, 15, 17, 20, 36, 40, 41, 43, 49, 50, 51, 54, 82, 83

Lang Peaks **61**
Le Casque **74**
Lenggrieser Ryggen **70**
Lennox **58**
Leo Glacier 53
Leutkirchner Tinde **70**
Lindauer Hornli **70**
Linne Gletscher 14, 26
Liverpool Coast 9
Liverpool Land 9, 89
Maclear **62**
Magdalene **65**
Magog **64**
Main Glacier 18, 40, 46
Majorpasset (see Col Major)
Malmberg 11, 23, 24, 41, 82, 83
Mars Glacier 18
Mellem Gletscher 23, 24
Mellem Pass 23, 24, 49, 52, **78**
Menanders Islands 25, 49, 94
Merchiston (Merchistontinde) 19, 37, 44, 51, **58**
Mercury Glacier 18, 39, 40, 84
Mesters Vig 10, 11, 13, 21–25, 33–53, 84, 88, 92–94
Midnight Peak **62**
Mittenwalder Tinde **70**
Mitterspids 35, **57**
Molehill **74**
Mont Blanc de Furesö 51, **75**
Mont Frendo 50, **74**
Mont Saussure **68**
Muhldorfer Spids **70**
Munchner Tinde **69**
Murchison Bjerge 14, 82
Mythotinde 52, **76**
Nathorsts Land 26, 27, 38, 50, 86, 87, 88, 90
Neptune Glacier 84, 85
Nevis **63**, 84
Newnham Col 15, 17, 42, **81**, 84
Newnham Tump **64**
Nordvest Fjord 9, 13, 18, 37, 52, 53, 84
Noret 23

Norsketinde   14, 18, 26, 34, 35, 50, 52, **55**, 82, 85
Notting Hill   44, **67**
Orion-Borgbjerg Col   53, **81**, 84
Orion Glacier   18, 40, 53
Ostre Gletscher   23
Panoramic Peak   47, **72**
Pegasus Glacier   40
Pembroke   42, **64**
Pevensey   **60**
Piccadilly   **66**
Pic A. Georges   50, 51, **74**
Pic Andersen   50, **74**
Pic Flotard   **75**
Pic Ludovica   50, **74**
Pictet Bjerge   9
Pimlico   **66**
Pinnacle   **74**
Pisa   **62**
Piz Coaz   **68**
Piz Dominant   **69**
Piz Spescha   **68**
Piz Vadian   **68**
Pleinting Bjerg   **69**
Plinganser Col   **80**
Point 1750m. (Vikingebrae)   **72**
Point 2250m. (Friheds Gletscher) 50, **72**
Pointe d'Argent   **75**
Pointe Humbert   51, **75**
Pointe Michel Gravost   **76**
Point Neurose   41, **61**
Pollux Glacier   16, 47
Poplar   **66**
Priener Kalotte   **70**
Priener Spids   **70**
Prinsesse Gletscher   10, 13, 16, 20, 47, 50, 51, 84
Proctor's Pinnacle   **65**
Prometheus   40, **63**
Purtscheller Tinde   **72**
Pyramid Peak   45, **68**
Queenstinde   43, **64**
Richmond   44, **67**
Rommelshausener Spids   **70**
Roscoe Bjerge   53

Roslinborg   37, 46, **59**
Roslin Gletscher   13, 15–18, 20, 37, 42, 46, 49, 52–54, 84
Royal Peak   19, 41, 44, **60**, 82
Ruthven   37, 45, **58**
Sabine Island   32
Sand Gletscher   86, 87
Santes Fair   41, 61
Saturn Glacier   18, 22
Schaffhauserdal   26, 86–88
Schneekuppe   47, **72**
Schuchert Dal   9–11, 13, 17, 18, 23, 24, 39, 49, 52–54, 89, 92–94
Schuchert Gletscher   13, 16, 17, 20, 23, 24, 33, 41, 43, 51, 83
Schuchert-Gully Col   **80**
Scoresby Land   9–11, 25, 32, 33
Scoresby Sound   9, 10, 32, 84, 89, 92
Scoresbysund   10, 32, 53, 84
Sedgwick Gletscher   14, 26
Sefstromsgipfel   20, 35, **57**, 83
Sefstroms Glacier   13–15, 17, 19, 26, 27, 35–39, 42, 43, 45, 51 83, 94
Sefstromstinde   15, 19, 28, 35, 37, 45, 50, **56**
Sefstroms-Lang Col   **80**
Selwyn   **65**
Sendlinger Bjerg   **71**
Sendlinger Kalotte   **71**
Sentinel   40, **61**
Sidney   42, **64**
Sidneytinde   **71**
Silberspitzen (Silver Peaks)   **69**
Skeldal   9, 13, 22, 36, 83, 93
Skel River   22, 25, 36
Skel Glacier   16, 22, 23, 36, 51
Skel Pass   16, 23, 33, 40, 43, 51, **78**
Skiferbjerg   **56**
Skipperdal   25
Skoldungebrae   13, 14, 25, 34, 43, 48
Slanstinde   **76**
Smalle Gletscher   87

Index of place names in Greenland

Snetoppen   15, 19, 42, **64**
Solvhorn   34, **55**
Sonnblickspids   36, **57**
Sortjehorn   23
Spörre Gletscher   13, 16, 17, 20, 27, 37, 40, 45–47, 84
St Bartholomew's Tower   **66**
St John's Peak   **65**
Staunings Alps   9–11, 13, 15 et seq
Steinbjerg   **70**
Stirling   **59**
Stor Gletscher   (see Lang Gletscher)
Strittbjerg   **69**
Stuttgarter Spids   **70**
Sun Valley Camp   36, 37, 48
Sussex   42, **64**, 85
Swiss Peak   33, 36, **55**, 83
Syd Kap   10, 37
Sydvest Gletscher   38, 86, 87
Syltoppen   25, 45, 82
Tantallon   20, 37, 45, **58**
Tantalus   **63**
Tarnfjeld   34, 38, 44, **55**
Taurubjerg   53, **76**
Taurus Glacier   40
Tent Peak   **63**
Thurweiser Kopf   **71**
Tintagel   39, **59**
Tioram   **59**
Tirefour   50, **73**
Tolzerspids   **69**
Toni Kurz Spids   **71**

Tour Carrée   **76**
Tour Chartreuse   51, **75**
Tour des Camaieux   **74**
Tour du Pavot   **75**
Tour Vercours   51, **75**
Trekant Gletscher   87, 88
Trespids   50, **72**
Treyarnon   **73**
Trinity   15, 19, 42, **64**, 83
Triton Glacier   84
Trumpington Col   17, 51, **79**
Tunatinde   49, **73**
Tunnelelv   22, 23, 94
Ulmer Spids   **70**
Uranus Glacier   52, 84, 85
Vardefjeld   34, **55**
Vauxhall   **66**
Vertebrae   15, 43
Vikingebrae 13–15, 26, 33, 34, 45, 50, 52, 53, 82, 89
Violin Gletscher   35, 86
Wapping   **67**
Wedge   **74**
Wedge Peak   40, 41, **63**
Weisse Wand   36, 45, **57**
Wellenkamp Spids   **71**
Werner Bjerge   9, 11, 23, 28, 33, 89, 90
Weydmannsburg   45, **68**
Wordie Pass   15, 43, **79**
Yllis   53, **77**
Zeus   **62**
Zuckerhutl   **71**
Zwerg Spids   **70**